The Museums of Ireland

The Museums of Ireland

A Celebration

Compiled and Edited by
The Liffey Press

The Liffey Press

Published by
The Liffey Press Ltd
Ashbrook House
10 Main Street
Raheny, Dublin 5, Ireland
www.theliffeypress.com

A catalogue record of this book is
available from the British Library.

ISBN 1-904148-88-3

Printed in Spain by Graficas Cems.

Contents

Foreword, *by Dr Hugh Maguire, The Heritage Council*   viii

The Museums of Connaught

Dartfield—Ireland's Horse Museum   3

Derryglad Folk Museum   5

The Famine Museum   9

King House Interpretive Galleries and Museum   13

The Model Arts and Niland Gallery   17

National Museum of Ireland, Country Life   21

Sligo Folk Park   24

The Museums of Leinster

Bank of Ireland Arts Centre   29

Berkeley Costume and Toy Museum   31

Chester Beatty Library   33

County Carlow Military Museum   36

County Museum Dundalk   39

Dublin City Gallery The Hugh Lane   43

Dublin Writers Museum   49

Dublinia and the Viking World   52

Dublin's City Hall – The Story of the Capital   55

Fry Model Railway   58

The GAA Museum   60

Gallery of Photography   63

Ireland's Historic Science Centre   65

Irish Agricultural Museum   69

Irish Fly Fishing and Game Shooting Museum   71

Irish Jewish Museum   74

Irish Museum of Modern Art   77

CONTENTS

James Joyce Museum	81
Locke's Distillery Museum	83
Malahide Castle	85
National Gallery of Ireland	87
National Museum of Ireland, Archaeology and History	91
National Museum of Ireland, Decorative Arts and History	93
National Museum of Ireland, Natural History	97
Number Twenty-Nine	99
Pearse Museum	104
Shaw Birthplace	107
The Steam Museum	109

The Museums of Munster

Bunratty Castle and Folk Park	113
Cape Clear Museum and Archive	116
Celtic & Prehistoric Museum	118
Clare County Musuem	121
Cobh Museum	124
Cork Butter Museum	126
Craggaunowen, The Living Past	129
Crawford Municipal Art Gallery	133
Foynes Flying Boat Museum	137
The Hunt Museum	141
Irish Palatine Museum	144
Kerry County Museum	147
Lewis Glucksman Gallery	151
Limerick City Gallery of Art	155
Limerick Museum	157
Sirius Arts Centre	159
Waterford County Museum	162
Waterford Museum of Treasures	164

The Museums of Ulster

Armagh County Museum	169
Ballycastle Museum	172
Belfast Exposed Photography	175
Carrickfergus Museum	179

Contents

Cavan County Museum   181

Coleraine Museum   183

Donegal County Museum   185

Down County Museum   187

Downpatrick Railway Museum   191

Fermanagh County Museum   193

The Glebe House and Gallery   197

Gray Printer's Museum   200

Green Lane Museum   202

Larne Museum, Carnegie Centre and Arts   205

Millennium Court Arts Centre   207

Museum of the Master Saddler   211

Naughton Gallery at Queen's   213

Sheelin Irish Lace Museum, Fermanagh   217

Tower Museum and La Trinidad Valencera   219

Ulster American Folk Park   223

Ulster Folk and Transport Museum   226

Ulster Museum   229

W5 Science Centre   233

*"Museums do not just happen.
Numerous dedicated people
contribute time, thought,
energy, work — and above all,
expertise and talent . . ."*

— Paul Getty

Foreword

In reviewing the museums highlighted in this guide the reader and user will be struck by the diversity and geographical spread of collections across the island of Ireland. Museums accommodate collections as varied as the pots and pans of some long-gone farmhouse or the wonders of flying boats. Individual museum sites, as at the Ulster Folk and Transport Museum, address a complexity and array of themes that tell many, and sometimes contradictory, narratives. What may not be apparent in the lucidity of individual entries is the sheer commitment of many individuals to saving and caring for collections. These objects in their care provide tangible records of all aspects of our intertwined cultural heritages on this island. Similarly, what may not be apparent in the text, although the text itself is a welcome indicator of a change, are the many transformations underway across the Irish museum landscape. Gone are the days when a few poorly written labels stuck on with safety pins indicated to the visitor what was actually on view. Also consigned to the scrap-heap is the concept of the museum as a refuge from the present. Instead the best of today's museums confront the present, constantly interrogate the past, and provide pointers to where the future might lead. In that they are closer to the original meaning of the word "muse" than they have been for some time.

Few Irish museums receive direct State funding, although many do receive direct funding from local authorities. Many receive indirect support through financial aid for development and one-off projects, limited acquisition or under public employment and training programmes. Most benefit occasionally from State-funded agencies as with the Heritage Council's annual grants round. While this helps mostly small-scale projects, others of national significance have received significant funding over a number of years. The Council's support for the conservation of historic fifteenth-century vestments in Waterford Museum of Treasures would be a case in point. The United Kingdom's Accreditation Scheme has allowed Northern Ireland's museums to apply for much public funding. Typically, support from the UK's Heritage Lottery Fund has facilitated development plans for the Mid-Antrim Museums Service. Many more museums, some not within the remit of this publication, exist through the sheer dedication of volunteers and collectors, together with local community groups. Most give of their time freely and bring an enthusiasm and joy to their particular collections that is not always easy to replicate in larger institutions. How we bridge the gap between the professionalism of the larger institution and the enthusiastic warmth of the small-scale ones remains a challenge for the times ahead.

The museums listed in this guide are differentiated from their European counterparts in that they exist within different political jurisdictions, modes of regulation and funding. But fortunately this has not been a particular disadvantage. Indeed it has the potential to encourage a range of positive engagements with questions of cultural identity and debate over the norms and identities of heritages on the island. Organisations such as the Irish Museums Association work to provide support for professionals working in the sector across Ireland. The Northern Ireland Museums Council has supported a number of cross-border projects such as its "Training Needs Audit " (2004) and subsequent training indicatives and workshops. Although temporarily in abeyance, the NIMC and Heritage Council supported the Museum of the Year Awards that not only highlighted positive trends in the sector but also could withstand international scrutiny. The Chester Beatty Library, winner of the Museum of the Year Award in 2001, was European Museum of the Year in the following year. Small budgets did not necessarily mean limited imagination as reflected in the internationally awarded website for Waterford County Museum.

While there is much that is positive on the Irish museum stage there remain many areas of concern. There is a need to develop nationally considered collections policies to make sure that whole areas of our tangible heritage are available to be viewed and studied. Conversely some hard decisions may need to be made about a surfeit of other particular collection types. There is a need for more proactive preventive conservation as a front-line defence in caring for collections. The employment of professionally trained conservators in Irish museums lags behind other developed economies and needs to be promoted, as does the development of museums in cities or subject areas that are currently neglected. The ongoing maintenance and support of small local, and usually seasonal, museums is particularly uncertain. Volunteer groups achieve much but then there may be no culture of continuity in place when volunteers step down. The ownership of collections is often unclear with no clear distinction between what is owned by an individual or a group, as is often the case with the collections owned by local history societies. All too often in the rush of enthusiasm to put objects on display insufficient care is given to the long-term welfare of the particular object. It was with such concerns in mind that some years ago the Heritage Council embarked on the development of its Standards

& Accreditation Scheme for the Irish museum sector. While limited in its remit to the Republic of Ireland it nonetheless complemented existing schemes in Northern Ireland. Through a series of well-considered pilot projects and with the best available expertise the Council's scheme addresses the needs of collections first and foremost. Through a series of indicators museums, both small-scale and large-scale and in an entirely voluntary capacity, will be able to target all aspects of their operations for improvement, from front-of-house facilities to behind-the-scenes care and storage. The development of strategic thinking will be essential. The scheme being rolled out nationally in 2006 is further enhanced by the development of a training programme being delivered electronically by the University of Ulster. This course not only addresses the specific needs of the Irish museum sector, but will also allow a whole new generation of museum professionals to receive training on a par with the best available elsewhere.

Government departments are increasingly aware of the positive contribution the cultural sector makes to the wider society, not only through fostering an enhanced sense of place but in generating tourism revenue. For the outside visitor museums are well placed to provide windows into the heart of a community, not only a place for historic collections but also a guide to the diverse flora and fauna of any locality. For locals in turn museums can act as a community forum, a shared space for all, in which the past is a gateway to our present and the future negotiated, and issues of social inclusion and cultural diversity can be addressed fruitfully and creatively.

The publication of this guide is a welcome contribution to the professionalisation of the sector. It bears witness to the many dedicated staff and volunteers who share enthusiasm and scholarship with a wide variety of visitors, local and international. Its publication comes at a time when the Heritage Council's aspirations for the sector, long in gestation, will actually take flight. It is to be anticipated that there will be even more entries in future editions, all acting as custodians of the surprising breadth and richness of Ireland's tangible heritage.

Dr Hugh Maguire
Museums and Archives
The Heritage Council
April 2006

Acknowledgements

*T*he *Museums of Ireland: A Celebration* is intended to showcase the quality and breadth of museums and galleries on the island of Ireland. The information and images for each museum came from the museums themselves, primarily in response to a questionnaire sent out in autumn 2005. It is therefore advisable to check prices and opening times with the museums before visiting. We apologise to any museums that were inadvertently overlooked, or who for a variety of reasons were not able to send us the material required, and would be more than willing to include them in future editions of this book.

We would like to thank the Irish Museums Association for their assistance in this publication; thank you to Dr Hugh Maguire of the Heritage Council for writing the Foreword; thank you to the curators/owners of Number Twenty-Nine, the Lewis Glucksman Gallery, the Irish Fly Fishing and Game Shooting Museum, and the Derryglad Folk Museum for submitting thoughtful responses to our question, "Why museums?"; and thank you to all the museums who contributed material to this publication.

David Givens
Publisher
April 2006

The Museums of Connaught

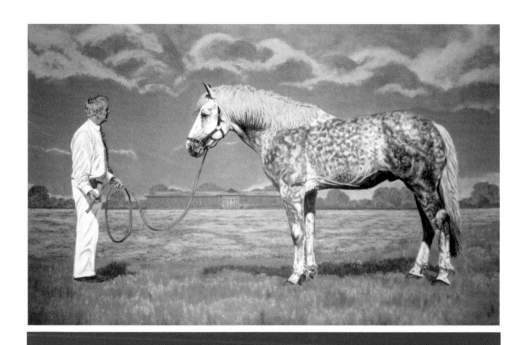

Dartfield —
Ireland's Horse World

Contact Information

Kilrickle, Loughrea
Co. Galway
Tel: 091 843968
Email: info@dartfieldhorsemuseum.com
Web: www.dartfieldhorsemuseum.com

Opening Hours

Open daily year round from
9.30 to 6.00
Admission: Adults, €7.00; Children/
Seniors, €4.50; Family, €16.00

Facilities

Café
Gift shop
Wheelchair access

How to Find Us

Located on the main Dublin–
Galway Road, N6, four miles
from Loughrea.

The galleries at Dartfield, Ireland's Horse World, house an informative display of exhibits highlighting the contribution of the horse to society from the earliest times to present day. Visitors can discover a forgotten world where society relied on the gentle pace of the horse in years gone by.

The founder of the museum, Willie Leahy, is a well-known Irish horseman and the largest breeder of Connemara ponies in the world. He also runs Connemara and coast trail riding holidays and is a field master of the Galway Blazers.

Dartfield is set amidst 350 acres of private land and is a perfect location to escape the hustle and bustle for a day. Children are especially catered for with an extensive array of toys, games, rocking horses and, of course, pony rides.

Highlights from the Collection

Highlights include the Galway Blazers room, which houses coats, jackets, saddles, etc which belonged to the founders of one of the most

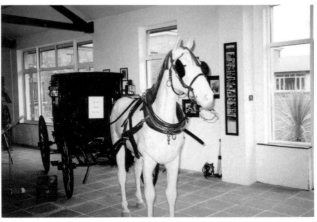

Exhibit Gallery One

famous hunts. Also on display is a brougham carriage dating from the 1800s which belonged to the American actress Lily Langtry.

Additional Information

Other activites at Dartfield include archery, clay-pigeon shooting, a treasure hunt, horse-drawn carriage rides, guided farm walks, a working sheepdog demonstration, riding a mechanical horse and more. Dartfield also hosts national/international horse trials, hunter trials and point-to-point races.

Evolution of the Horse Display

Derryglad Folk Museum

Contact Information

Derryglad, Curraghboy,
Athlone, Co. Roscommon
Tel: 090 6488192
Email: folkmuseum@unison.ie

Opening Hours

May to September, Monday to
Saturday, 10.00 to 6.00,
Sunday, 2.00 to 6.00
Admission fees: **Adult,** €5.00;
Seniors, €4.50; Children, €3.50;
Family, €15.00

Facilities

Gift shop
Wheelchair access

How to Find Us

From Athlone take the Tuam Road.
From Roscommon take the
Curraghboy Road.

No trip to the midlands is complete without a visit to Derryglad Folk Museum, situated in a rural setting in the heart of South Roscommon's unspoiled and unexplored countryside. Here in a friendly relaxed atmosphere visitors can view over 4,000 items dealing with history, heritage and folk culture. This all-weather facility deals with farm and folk life and includes horse-drawn machinery, tradesman's tools, old-style 1930s thatched bar and grocery, phonographs, gramaphones, radios, quern stones, rare bog butter, sundials, rush lights, a new display on Old Days, Old Ways at school with slates, slate pencils, dip pens, ink and blotting paper.

The MacCormac Photography Room displays the contents of an extensive photographic collection from 1948 to 2002 and includes items from

Photography Section

studios, darkrooms, finishing room, D&P line, cameras, enlargers, B&W and colour processing equipment, all on permanent display in a work-like setting.

1890 Barn Thresher

Why Museums?

"Museums are safe, secure repositories for the artefacts which make up the material history of a community or nation. The increasing pace of modern life and the displacement of people from their locality and ancestral way of life has greatly increased the value of museums to society. They help us to study our past and help build a deeper understanding of our present-day society."

— Charlie Finneran,
Derryglad Folk Museum

"Every view of the world that becomes extinct, every culture that disappears, diminishes a possibility of life."

— Octavio Paz

The Famine Museum

Contact Information

Strokestown Park
Co. Roscommon
Tel: 078 33013
Email: info@strokestownpark.ie
Web: www.strokestownpark.ie

Opening Hours

Open daily, 17 March to 31 October,
10.00 to 5.30
Admission fees: **Adult**, €12.50;
School Students, €5.70; Family, €28.00

Facilities

Restaurant
Gift shop
Wheelchair access

How to Find Us

Strokestown Park is 14 miles from
Longford on the N5.

The Great Irish Famine of the 1840s is now regarded as the single greatest social disaster of nineteenth-century Europe. Between 1845 and 1850, when blight devastated the potato crop, in excess of two million people — almost one-quarter of the entire population — either died or emigrated. The Famine Museum, located in the original Stable Yards of Strokestown Park House, was designed to commemorate the history of The Great Irish Famine of the 1840s and in some way to balance the history of the "Big House".

Whereas the landlord class had the resources to leave an indelible mark on the landscape, the Irish tenants lived in poverty and nothing of a physical nature has survived to commemorate their lives. The Famine Museum uses the unique documents that were discovered in the estate office, dealing with the administration of the estate during the tenure of the Mahon family. This collection includes many haunting pleas from starving tenants on the estate and the response they received.

The museum also has a strong educational focus and seeks to create a greater awareness of the horrors of contemporary famine by demonstrating the link between the causes of the Great Irish Famine of the 1840s and the ongoing spectre of famine in the developing world

today. The Famine Museum was opened in 1994 by the then President of Ireland, Mary Robinson, when she said, "More than anything else, this Famine Museum shows us that history is not about power or triumph nearly so often as it is about suffering and vulnerability."

Layout of the Museum

The fact that nothing of a physical nature remains to represent the lives of the Irish tenants at the time of the

Famine underlines the importance of the documents and letters on display in the museum. The museum is divided into ten rooms:

Room 1 – The Ascendancy

Room 2 – The Land and People

Room 3 – The Potato

Rooms 4 and 5 – Poor Law and Relief

Room 6 – Video Room

Room 7 – Emigration

Room 8 – Eviction

Room 9 – Secret Societies

Room 10 – After the Great Irish Famine

The Gardens

In August 1997 the gates of Strokestown Park Walled Gardens were opened to the public, after a ten-year restoration project. The gardens had received little or no maintenance since the 1960s and therefore had been totally reclaimed by nature. Many of the original features have been restored including the croquet lawn, the lawn tennis court, the summer house and a magnificent ornamental lily pond.

The herbaceous border is listed in *The Guinness Book of Records* as the longest herbaceous border in Britain and Ireland. It truly is breathtaking, having been planted in a rainbow colour scheme. Other equally beautiful features in the garden include a formal rose garden, a wonderful pergola, a wildflower garden and a fernery, to name but a few.

The Gardens at Strokestown Park

"Every great work of art has two faces, one towards its own time and one toward the future, toward eternity."

— Daniel Barenboim

King House Interpretive Galleries and Museum

Contact Information

Main Street
Boyle, Co. Roscommon
Tel: 071 9663242
Email: kinghouse@roscommoncoco.ie
Web: www.kinghouse.ie

Opening Hours

Open daily 1 April to 30 September,
10.00 to 6.00
Admission fees: **Adult**, €7.00;
Students/Seniors, €5.00;
Children, €4.00; Family, €18.00

Facilities

Restaurant
Gift shop
Wheelchair access

How to Find Us

Located in town centre just off the N4
Dublin–Sligo road.

King House is a magnificently restored Georgian mansion built around 1730 by Sir Henry King whose family was one of the most powerful and wealthy in Ireland. The grand scale of the reception gallery, its original stone floor, tripartite windows and high vaulted ceiling portray the impression that the house was built as a symbol of the status and power of the King family. After its first life as a home, King House became a military barracks to the famous Connaught Rangers from 1788 until 1922. In more recent years King House has also been a barracks for the Irish Army. Even today there remains an Army presence as the Reserve Defence Force are based in the West Wing of the House.

Highlights from the Collection

King House was built as a family home and the collection includes original paintings and family heirlooms from the descendants of the

King House from Pleasure Gardens

King family, including an eighteenth-century evening gown and coronet.

The Fighting Men from Connaught exhibition tells the story of King House from its time as a military barracks for the Connaught Rangers and their military campaigns around the world, including the Crimean and First World Wars. The Connaught Rangers Association Museum collection includes original artefacts and photographic images that focus on the many campaigns in the First World War. A newly opened Room of Rememberance commemorates the men who served in the ranks of that great regiment.

The Arts at King House

King House is home to the Boyle Civic Collection, widely considered as one of the finest collections of contemporary Irish paintings and sculpture. The objectives of the Trustees of the Civic Collection are to build a major col-

The Long Gallery

lection of Irish Art for the people of Boyle, thus enriching the community, and to make art more accessible to a wide variety of people. Decisions to acquire works for the collection are made by the Trustees led by a local business, Ahern & Co, and this co-operation with King House led to the Boyle Civic Collection being awarded the Allianz/Business2arts award in 2004 for best collaboration between a small business, as well as being Highly Commended for the Best Business/Arts Collaboration in the Community. The ever-expanding collection now comprises over 150 works and the majority of these are on permanent view in King House during opening hours.

In July of each year, the Festival Office for the Boyle Arts Festival is based in the Long Gallery and King House is the venue for many of the events including the main Visual Arts Exhibition. The festival programme also includes classical, jazz and tra-

ditional music, making use of the Roscommon County Council Steinway Piano. King House also hosts Boyle Arts Festival events on a year-round basis.

The Jail Cells

New Developments

The construction of a walkway through the attic of the house connects the "House of Kings" on the second floor to a new state of the art auditorium, with audiovisual presentation in the West Wing of the building.

Education Programmes

King House provides a range of educational resources which includes an in-depth historical project linked to the national curriculum. For further details contact the Educational Development Officer or see www.kinghouse.ie.

Connaught Rangers Collection

"My mother said to me, 'If you become a soldier, you'll be a general; if you become a monk, you'll end up the pope.' Instead, I became a painter and wound up as Picasso."

— Pablo Picasso

The Model Arts and Niland Gallery

Contact Information

The Mall
Sligo
Tel: 071 9141405
Email: info@modelart.ie
Web: www.modelart.ie

Opening Hours

Open Tuesdays to Sundays
Admission is free to the galleries

Facilities

Café
Gift shop
Wheelchair access

How to Find Us

Located on the Mall in Sligo town.

Certainly one of the most stylish arts centres in Ireland, this beautiful building alone is worth the trip to Sligo. Following a stunning renovation in 2000 it now houses an exciting programme of visual art, performance, music, film, comedy and arts education; something for everyone every day of the week.

The Niland Art collection, housed here, contains over 250 pieces by important Irish contemporary artists including Estella Solomons, Louis le Brocquy, George Russell, and John and Jack B. Yeats among others. Permanently housed at the Model, a selection from the collection is exhibited in four cycles each year. The

The Atrium (Grey Wall)

acclaimed contemporary exhibition programme features nine solo or group exhibitions annually, drawn from the best of local, national and international artists. Previous exhibitors have included Vivienne Roche,

John Shinnors, Barrie Cooke, Bernadette Kiely and Camille Souter.

The Model Niland also screens art house films each week in association with the Sligo Film Society and plays host to a number of festivals all year round, including the Sligo Festival of Baroque Music, Scríobh Literary Festival, Sligo Contemporary Music Festival, and Solo, a festival of the solo performer.

Highlights from the Collection

The Niland Gallery is called after one of Sligo's most dedicated and hard-working citizens — Nora Niland. In the 1950s, Niland was instrumental in establishing the Sligo Municipal Art Collection, which today bears her name.

Niland was appointed Sligo County Librarian in 1945 and she was quick to spot the untapped potential of the Yeats connection with Sligo. Due to her boundless enthusiasm and determination, Niland found herself planning the first International Yeats Summer School in 1958. She hit upon the idea of borrowing five works by Jack B. Yeats, from the Capuchin Annual in Dublin, to exhibit for the duration of the summer school. These works consisted of three large oil paintings, *Communicating with Prisoners*, *The Funeral of Harry Boland*, and *The Island Funeral*, along with two smaller watercolours, *Market Day*, and *The Star Gazer*.

Over the course of the exhibition, Niland came to believe that these paintings would make a great permanent addition to the cultural hub of Sligo, and set about raising the £3,000 needed to purchase them. Although it took her two years, Niland's dogged determination ensured that the paintings remained in Sligo and formed the nucleus of what has now become the Niland Collection.

During the course of her fundraising, Niland made some invaluable contacts, not least of whom was James Healy. Healy was the New York-born son of Irish immigrants, and had amassed a great fortune on the stock exchange. Both he and his wife, Josephine, had a passion for the west of Ireland and were avid collectors of Irish art. Between 1965 and 1966, Healy generously gave Nora Niland donations of almost thirty paintings in memory of his parents John and Catherine Healy. In 1975, after the death of his wife, Healy donated her entire collection of modern Irish art, consisting of 35 works, to the Sligo Municipal Collection. This bequest contained works by Maurice McGonigal, Sean Keating and Paul Henry.

Educational Programmes

The Model has a vibrant educational programme which caters for adults and children alike. Highlights of the programme include life drawing for adults, film making and animation for teens and art for children.

The Model's interior is full of light

"We can learn from history how past generations thought and acted, how they responded to the demands of their time and how they solved their problems."

— Gerda Lerner

National Museum of Ireland Country Life

Contact Information

Turlough Park
Castlebar, Co. Mayo
Tel: 094 9031755
Email: tpark@museum.ie
Web: www.museum.ie

Opening Hours

Tuesday to Saturday,
10.00 to 5.00
Sunday, 2.00 to 5.00
Admission is free.

Facilities

Café
Gift shop
Wheelchair access

How to Find Us

Located just outside Turlough Village, on the N5 just four miles east of Castlebar.

The National Museum of Ireland — Country Life is the latest addition to the National Museum of Ireland and is the first branch of the National Museum to be situated outside Dublin. The Museum opened to the public in September 2001. The exhibitions portray the lives of ordinary people who lived in rural Ireland in the period 1850–1950. Emphasis is placed on the continuity of lifestyles that were established for several hundred years and which lasted well into the twentieth century.

The museum is situated in the grounds of Turlough Park House a short distance from the town of Castlebar, Co. Mayo. Turlough Park House was built by Charles Lionel Fitzgerald in 1865. The house has been fully restored and serves as the main office as well as the education/reception area and is used to show visitors how families like its original owners lived. The house was designed in the High Victorian Gothic style by Thomas Newenham Deane, who was responsible for designing the National Museum of Archaeology and History on Kildare Street, Dublin. Charles Lionel Fitzgerald also developed the extensive gardens in the grounds of Turlough Park and undertook improvements to the agricultural land farmed by tenants. In the park, located not far from the artificial lake (*turloch* in Irish, from which the area takes its name), is the site of the castle built by the Anglo-Norman de Burgo family.

The purpose-built exhibition gallery, designed by the Architectural Service of the Office of Public Works, is a four-storey curved, stone-clad

National Museum of Ireland — Country Life

block set into the terraces of the gardens leading to the artificial lake. A large storage area and modern conservation facilities are located close to the new building.

In 2002, the National Museum of Ireland — Country Life was presented with an Interpret Ireland Award for recognition of its "excellent interpretative practice contributing to greater awareness and understanding of Ireland's Heritage". In the same year it also received the prestigious title of "Museum of the Year" which was awarded jointly by the Gulbenkian Foundation and the Heritage Council of Ireland, in association with the Northern Ireland Museums Council.

The National Museum of Ireland — Country Life is home to the Irish Folklife Division. This Division is responsible for the care of the National Folklife Collection which comprises over 50,000 objects. These collections reflect Irish traditional life, largely of a rural nature, and include objects dealing with agriculture, fishing and hunting, clothing, architecture, vernacular furniture, trades and crafts, transport, sports and leisure and religion.

Education Programme

The Museum of Country Life runs programmes for adults, families and schools to raise awareness of the Museum collection and the associated traditional crafts, customs and traditions. The programmes consist of talks, demonstrations and performances as well as hands-on art and craft workshops. Groups can arrange a tailored programme for their visit. Admission to events is free but booking is required.

The rear view balancing act, early twentieth-century transport in the west

Sligo Folk Park

Contact Information

Riverstown
Co. Sligo
Tel: 071 9165001
Email: sligofolkpark@eircom.net
Website: www.sligofolkpark.com

Opening Hours

Mid-April to October, Monday to
Saturday, 10.00 to 5.30;
Sunday 12.30 to 6.00
November to April, open by
appointment
Admission: Adults €5.00;
Children, €3.00

Facilities

Café
Gift shop
Wheelchair access

How to Find Us

Located in the village of Riverstown
just off the N4 road in east County
Sligo.

Sligo Folk Park is the largest tourist attraction of its kind in the north-west of Ireland. Here visitors can experience rural Irish heritage and culture from times gone by deep in the heart of Sligo.

Built in the style of a traditional courtyard, the Museum and Exhibition Hall contain one of Ireland's finest collections of rural history and artefacts. Inside the village hall is a carefully recreated village streetscape consisting of a variety of shops and services which were part and parcel of every Irish village – the creamery store, the pub, the grocers, each containing authentic objects.

Highlights of the Collection

Included within Sligo Folk Park is a traditional cottage named Mrs

Sligo Folk Park

Buckley's Cottage, as well as Mill-view House, which originates from the late nineteenth century and is surrounded by open workshops in which historical artefacts are restored to their former glory.

Other attractions include a fully equipped forge, a replicated classroom, a complete range of restored agricultural implements, plus geese, turkeys, peacocks, rabbits, goats, hens and ducks.

Exploring Sligo Folk Park

The Museums of Leinster

Bank of Ireland Arts Centre

Contact Information

Foster Place
Off Dame Street
Dublin 2
Tel: 01 6712261
Email: boi.arts@boimail.com
Web: www.boi.ie/artscentre

Opening Hours

Tuesday to Friday, 9.30 to 4.00
Saturday, 11.00 to 4.00
Admission fees: **Adult,** €5.00;
Students, €3.00

Facilities

Coffee shop

How to Find Us

Located beside 2 College Green, off
Dame Street, on the edge of Temple
Bar.

The Bank of Ireland Arts Centre & Museum in Foster Place presents "200 Years of History", an interactive display which reflects both Irish history and the history of banking over the past 200 years. It also traces the history of the adjoining College Green building, one of the architectural landmarks of Georgian Dublin, dating back to its former role as the Irish Houses of Parliament. Known as the "The Liberator", The Daniel O'Connell exhibition tells the story of his life and follows his championing of the cause of political change though constitutional means.

his death mask and various decorative artefacts connected with his life.

New Developments/ Future Plans

Future plans include updates to the Timeline Room to reflect recent world events, and extension of the

Mace of the Irish Houses of Parliament 1765-1800

Highlights from the Collection

The highlights of the Arts Centre Museum and tour include the Mace of the Irish House Commons, which sat in the College Green Parliament between 1765 and 1800; the Model of 2 College Green circa 200 years ago; authentic ledgers which form part of the Archive, some of which are on display to the public; and The Daniel O'Connell Exhibition Room, which includes three portraits of O'Connell,

Tours Programme to younger school children of 10-12 years, which is currently in development.

Educational/ Special Programmes

The Museum tour will be of special interest to people with an interest in architecture, history and business/ economics. Junior Certificate and Leaving Certificate students will also be interested in the museum as the material links into the exam curriculum.

Berkeley Costume and Toy Museum

Contact Information

Berkeley Forest
New Ross, Co Wexford
Tel: 051 421361

Opening Hours

Open May to October
Groups only by appointment
Admission is €6.00

How to find us

Located 2.5 miles from New Ross on the Enniscorthy Road. Turn right at the "Berkeley Forest" sign and go another 300 metres to the house.

The Berkeley Costume and Toy Museum consists of a private collection of costume and toys dating from 1750 to 1924. It is housed in the former drawing room and dining room of this late eighteenth-century house. The property formed the estate of the family of George Berkeley, the well-known eighteenth-century Irish philosopher.

The exhibits include silk court dresses of an Irish provenance, eighteenth-century wooden dolls and a good cross-section of Victorian costumes and toys. There is also a handsome dollhouse, lavishly furnished.

Highlights from the Collection

The museum contains several sack-back eighteenth century gowns; a

Some early nineteenth century costumes

rare Irish gentleman's suit, 1790; an eighteenth-century wooden doll; a rocking horse of unusually large dimensions; a collection of hats and bonnets from 1780 to 1910; ladies' embroidered shoes; and a Palladian-style dollhouse, 1860.

New Developments

Berekeley Forest House is a protected building and a private home. Visitor numbers are therefore necessarily restricted. However, plans are underway to expand visiting possibilities, both inside and outside the house.

Additional Information

All tours are personally guided by the proprietor, Countess Ann Bernstorff. Catering can be organised for large groups and the gardens of the house are available for picnics.

Eighteenth century Queen Anne doll

The Chester Beatty Library

Contact Information

Dublin Castle
Dublin 2
Tel: 01 4070750
Email: info@cbl.ie
Website: www.cbl.ie

Opening Hours

Monday to Friday, 10.00 am to 5.00 pm
(May to September)
Tuesday to Friday, 10.00 am to 5.00 pm
(October-April)
Saturdays, 11.00 to 5.00 (all year)
Sundays, 1.00 to 5.00 (all year)
Closed public holidays.
Admission is free.

Facilities

Restaurant
Gift and Book Shop
Audio-visual presentations
Roof Garden
Wheelchair access

How to Find Us

Located Off Dame St, behind City
Hall, ten minutes' walk from Trinity
College en route to Christ Church
Cathedral.

Situated in the heart of Dublin city centre, the Chester Beatty Library is an art museum and library which houses a great collection of manuscripts, miniature paintings, prints, drawings, rare books and some decorative arts assembled by Sir Alfred Chester Beatty (1875–1968). The Library's exhibitions open a window on the artistic treasures of the great cultures and religions of the world. Its rich collection from countries across Asia, the Middle East, North Africa and Europe offers visitors a visual feast. Chester Beatty Library was named Irish Museum of the Year in 2000 and was awarded

Elephant Treatise, AD 1816, Thailand

the title European Museum of the Year in 2002, a coveted international accolade in the museum world.

Collections of The Chester Beatty Library

The Library's collections are displayed in two permanent exhibitions: "Sacred Traditions" and "Artistic Traditions".

The "Sacred Traditions" Gallery exhibits the sacred texts, illuminated manuscripts and miniature paintings from the great religions and systems of belief represented in the collections — Christianity, Islam and Buddhism with smaller displays on Confucianism, Daoism, Sikhism and Jainism. The Biblical Papyri, the remarkable collection of Qur'an

Islamic Section, Sacred Traditions Gallery

manuscripts and scrolls and books of Buddhist thought provide the focus for the displays. Audiovisual programmes on rites of passage in many faiths, prayer and pilgrimage enhance the displays.

The "Artistic Traditions" gallery is devoted mainly to works of art on paper, techniques of print-making, binding and paper-making and the art of miniature painting. The display draws on the rich manuscript holdings, the collection of rare printed books and of decorative arts, especially from East Asia. The exhibition is introduced by a display devoted to the life and work of Sir Alfred Chester Beatty.

In addition to the items on display from its permanent collection, the Library mounts special temporary exhibitions. It also runs an event-filled public programme which includes lectures, workshops and demonstrations.

Education Programmes

Contact the Library for information on their Public Programme, including talks, demonstrations in techniques represented in the collection, such as calligraphy, painting, printing and other crafts, as well as public tours and films.

The Library hosts a series of monthly workshops for 7–11 year olds. Children can explore a wide range of exciting topics, from making lanterns celebrating the Chinese New Year to following the travels of explorers through the collection, as well as learning about a host of other cultures and religions.

God's Meeting with Shiva and Vishnu,
c.1850 AD, Pahari, India

County Carlow Military Museum

Contact Information

Old Church, Athy Road
Carlow Town
Tel: 087 2850509
Web: www.countycarlowmilitary
museum.com

Opening Hours

Open Sundays, from 2.00 to 5.00 pm
Group tours for other days and times
please contact us.
Admission fees: **Adult**, €2.50;
Children/Seniors, €1.30.

Facilities

Wheelchair access

How to Find Us

Located in the Old Church Building
in the grounds of St. Dympna's
Hospital on the Athy Road in
Carlow Town.

The County Carlow Military Museum is based in a late nineteenth-century church building. Founded in 1995, the Museum's emphasis is on Carlow's military history and Carlow soldiers. Currently the items in the Museum's collection cover the last 200 years of Carlow's military heritage. Some of the main displays are: Irish Army Reserve 1950-2005, Irish Air Corps, Great War, Medieval Soldier, Carlow Militia, Irish War of Independence and Civil War, Irish Soldiers with the United Nations in Lebanon, Somalia and the Congo, Captain Myles Kehoe and Weapons of the Irish soldier. There are many other displays and exhibits.

Irish Army Reserve Display

Highlights from the Collection

Highlights include the Drums of the 8th Militia Battalion Kings Royal Rifle Corps, The Dag Hammarskjöld

Irish in Lebanon

Medal and Military Star Medal from the Congo Display.

New Developments

New developments include an audio-visual display with newsreel footage of the Irish War of Independence and Civil War, as well as footage of the Irish Defence Forces during the 1930s. Future plans include exhibits on the 1798 Rebellion, World War II and expanding and upgrading current displays.

Educational Programmes

Work sheets are available for school tours and language school students.

"At a museum, there will be one person weeping in front of the Monet, another weeping in front of the Renoir and another weeping in front of the Picasso. Who can say what moves each person so?"

— Bebe Neuwirth

County Museum Dundalk

Contact Information

Jocelyn Street
Dundalk, Co Louth
Tel 042 9327056
Email: dlkmuseum1@eircom.net

Opening Hours

April to October, Monday to
Saturday, 10.30 to 5.30;
Sundays, 2.00 to 6.00
Admission fees: **Adult,** €3.80;
Students/Seniors, €2.50;
Children, €1.25

Facilities

Wheelchair access

How to Find Us

Located in Dundalk city centre.

The County Museum, Dundalk is one of Ireland's finest local authority museums. Opened in 1994 the museum is located in a lovingly restored eighteenth-century distillery. The distillery once boasted the tallest chimney in Ireland, but unfortunately could not draw smoke. The warehouse subsequently came in to the possession of the Carroll's Tobacco Group and was used as a bonded warehouse. With the gradual decline in global cigarette sales, the Carroll Group slowly scaled down their operation and presented Dundalk Urban District Council with the warehouse on condition that it be used for the purposes of an interpretative centre. Just nine years later it is one of the finest museums in the country boasting a variety of awards including two Gulbenkian Museum of the Year Awards (1995

Living History Display

and 1999) as well as several awards for the quality of its exhibition: Gold Award for the Best Commissioned Display (1995) and the Interpret Ireland Award (2000).

Highlights from the Collection

The museum boasts a variety of interesting artefacts, most notably a Heinkel bubble car located on the ground floor gallery as well as a leather coat reputed to have been worn by King William of Orange at the Battle of the Boyne. The Museum attempts to reflect the social, industrial and cultural life of County Louth and this objective is

Storytelling at the Museum

to be seen in the diverse nature of its collection. The Heinkel was the only car ever made in Ireland; many were assembled but the Heinkel was made in Dundalk. The story of King William's jacket (or jerkin to give it its proper title) is an interesting one. In July 2000 the Museum was approached by a private individual informing them that he had a leather coat which was reputed to have been worn by King William of Orange at the Battle of the Boyne. According to the individual the jacket had come to

his family's possession via his great grandfather. The jerkin is now in pride of place on the museum's first floor exhibition.

Educational Programmes

The museum's educational officer organises a variety of events throughout the year ranging from lectures to workshops. In addition there is an outreach service provided, which will facilitate groups who cannot visit the museum by bringing the collection to them.

View of Museum Reception

"We have a hunger of the mind which asks for knowledge of all around us, and the more we gain, the more is our desire; the more we see, the more we are capable of seeing."

— Maria Mitchell

Dublin City Gallery
The Hugh Lane

Contact Information

Charlemont House
Parnell Square North, Dublin 1
Tel: 01 2225550
Email: info.hughlane@dublincity.ie
Web: www.hughlane.ie

Opening Hours

Tuesday to Thursday, 9.30 to 6.00
Friday and Saturday, 9.30 to 5.00
Sunday, 11.00 to 5.00
Admission is free (cover charge to Francis Bacon Studio)

Facilities

Restaurant
Gift shop
Wheelchair access

How to Find Us

Located on Parnell Square North in the city centre.

Above: Walter Osborne,
Tea in the Garden

Dublin City Gallery, The Hugh Lane, one of Ireland's most historic galleries, more than doubled its size this year following a period of major expansion and refurbishment.

The €13 million expansion incorporated the construction of a new contemporary wing, spanning three floors and boasting 13 new galleries to complement the existing 9 galleries and the Francis Bacon Studio currently housed in Charlemont House, which has been the home of the Gallery on Parnell Square since 1933.

Interior of The Hugh Lane

Following the extensive project which doubled the exhibition space of the Gallery from 2,000 to 4,000 square metres (44,000 square feet),

Sean Scully

the Gallery has acquired several significant contemporary works by Irish and international artists, in excess of €11 million, from artists and benefactors. For the first time since 1913, all eight of Sir Hugh Lane's impressionist paintings, which are shared with the National Gallery in London, will hang together for a spectacular exhibition celebrating the opening of the new extension. The exhibition will include works by Manet, Monet, Renoir and Degas.

Barbara Dawson, Director of the Gallery, and her curators had a major input into the flow and feel of the "new" Gallery and worked closely with architects Gilroy McMahon and the Gallery's curators in shaping the gallery's exhibition identity.

The new Gallery is an extension behind the existing 1728 Charlemont

House building and allows the visitor to appreciate the Gallery's offering from the inside-out. The new Gallery has a natural flow from the main gallery and incorporates 13 new galleries, a dedicated educational and lecture room with state of the art equipment, a bookshop and a café.

Jack B. Yeats, There is no night

Exhibitions Calendar

First on the calendar for the Gallery relaunch is a major retrospective of the work of Brian O'Doherty/Patrick Ireland. Irish-born and US-based, he is a pioneering figure of Conceptualism and an artist of extraordinary range. He is renowned in particular for his Labyrinths and Rope Draw-

Elsworth Kelly,
Black Relief over Yellow and Orange

ings and was described by George Segal as "one of the great post-war drawing oeuvres". Trained as a medical doctor in University College Dublin and subsequently at Harvard University, O'Doherty was a major participant in the development of the Conceptual art movement.

The reopening also sees the launch of a permanent Sean Scully exhibition room, specially designed and dedicated to the acclaimed Irish artist. Widely regarded as the most important abstract artist of his generation, Sean Scully donated seven significant paintings to the Gallery, which can be viewed in his own exhibition area. An eighth piece, which completes the current exhibition collection, was donated by a member of the business community.

Not since the donation of the Francis Bacon Studio has the Gallery received such a gift, and as it will be the only one of its kind outside the US it is set to become an international focus for contemporary art in Dublin and a major visitor attraction.

The reopening also heralded the acquisition of six unfinished Bacon paintings. These works — previously on loan — combined with Francis Bacon's Studio, completed this most original insight into the artistic process ever seen in a museum context. These six canvases, worth €4 million, chart Bacon's career from the period of his first major breakthrough in the 1940s to the last years of his life when he had attained the status of the leading figurative artist of his time. They are unique among his paintings on public display since they are incomplete and thus reveal his unorthodox techniques in their raw state. The *Unfinished* paintings enhance the experience of the Studio by allowing the visitor to study Bacon's canvases in tandem with his workspace.

As part of the celebration of a refurbished O'Connell Street, Dublin City Gallery The Hugh Lane will curate an exhibition of large-scale bronze hares by the renowned sculptor Barry Flanagan. Ten will be temporarily sited from O'Connell Bridge to the Hugh Lane forecourt. The artist has had major exhibitions of his bronzes on Park Avenue, New York, in Chicago and in Seattle. This exhibition is in collaboration with the Irish Museum of Modern Art (IMMA). Flanagan's upcoming exhibition at IMMA provides a complementary context for this spectacular event and the joint project represents the first major collaboration between Dublin City Gallery The Hugh Lane and IMMA, running from 26 June to 30 October 2006.

Co-curated with Jens Hoffmann, Director of Exhibitions, Institute of

Jean Baptiste Camille Corot, The Punt

Contemporary Art in London, is an exhibition entitled The Studio, which will open in November and continue to February 2007. Inspired by the presence of the London studio of Francis Bacon, which is on permanent view at Dublin City Gallery the Hugh Lane, this exhibition sets out to investigate the role, the idea and function of the artist's studio as the main space of activity in the making and production of art. The Studio will look into the changes that the idea of the studio has endured over the last decades and ask whether or not the studio is in fact still the main sphere of creative production for artists at a moment when art has become increasingly idea-based and less and less dependent on the notion of skills.

The Studio will present a set of artworks by artists that directly addresses their relationship to the studio. The exhibition will include works by Andy Warhol, Daniel Buren, John Baldessari, Thomas Demand, Fischili and Weiss, Urs Fischer, Andrew Grassie, Paul McCarthy, Dieter Roth, Hans Schabus, Frances Stark, Wolfgang Tillmans and Ian Wallace, among others.

The Studio will also encompass organised weekly studio visits for the public to studios of artists living and working in Dublin. An interna-tional symposium on The Studio will be held in early 2007.

The Francis Bacon Studio remains a key feature of the Gallery with Dublin City Gallery The Hugh Lane acknowledged as the world centre for studies on Francis Bacon.

The Gallery continues to exhibit both historic and contemporary works from a range of artists including Jack B. Yeats, William Orpen, Degas, Lavery and Louis le Brocquy. Not seen since 1999, Harry Clarke's *Eve of Saint Agnes* stained glass masterpiece will make a welcome return to the gallery as part of the permanent collection.

Harry Clarke, Eve of St Agnes

"I want to give a picture of Dublin so complete that if the city suddenly disappeared from the earth it could be reconstructed out of my book."

— James Joyce, about Ulysses

Dublin Writers Museum

Contact Information

18 Parnell Square
Dublin 1
Tel: 01 8722077
Email: writers@dublintourism.ie
Web: www.writersmuseum.com

Opening Hours

Monday to Saturday, 10.00 to 5.00
Sunday and Holidays, 11.00 to 5.00
Admission fees: **Adult**, €6.70;
Children, €4.20; Family, €19.00

Facilities

Restaurant and coffee shop
Bookshop

How to Find Us

Located in Parnell Square in
the city centre.

The idea of a Dublin Writers Museum was originated by the journalist and author Maurice Gorham (1902–1975), who proposed it to Dublin Tourism. It was to take some years before a suitable building and a sufficient level of funding became available. Opened in November 1991 at No. 18, Parnell Square, the museum occupies an original eighteenth-century house, which accommodates the museum rooms, library, gallery and administration area.

The museum was established to promote interest, through its collection, displays and activities, in Irish literature as a whole and in the lives and works of individual Irish writers. Through its association with the Irish Writers' Centre it provides a link with living writers and the international literary scene. On a national level it acts as a centre, simultaneously pulling together the strands of Irish literature and complementing the smaller, more detailed museums devoted to individuals like Joyce, Shaw, Yeats and Pearse. It functions as a place where people can come from Dublin, Ireland and abroad to experience the phenomenon of Irish writing both as history and as actuality.

The writers featured in the museum are those who have made an important contribution to Irish or international literature or, on a local level, to the literature of Dublin. It is a view of Irish literature from a Dublin perspective.

In the two museum rooms a history of Irish literature from its beginnings up to recent times is presented. The panels describe the various phases, movements and notable names, while the showcases and pic-

Interior of Dublin Writers Museum

tures illustrate the lives and works of individual writers. Room 1 takes the story through to the end of the nineteenth century and the beginning of the literary revival. Room 2 is entirely devoted to the great writers of the twentieth century. Living writers, even those who have already established their place in history, are not included in the display.

At the top of the grand staircase is the Gorham Library with its Stapleton ceiling. Here is kept the museum's reserve of books, including rare and first editions and critical works. There are also displays of volumes from special collections.

Next to the library is the salon, known as The Gallery of Writers. This splendidly decorated room, with its portraits and busts of Irish writers, is used for exhibitions and special occasions.

On the ground floor is a corridor leading to the annexe. At the back of the building are the coffee shop and bookshop. The stairs lead up to the exhibition room on the first floor, where

Entrance to the Museum

temporary exhibitions are mounted, and Seomra na nÓg, the adjoining room which is devoted to children's literature. Upstairs on the second floor are the lecture rooms. Portraits and other pictures are displayed on walls throughout the annexe.

The museum collection is as fascinating as it is various. As might be expected, there are plenty of books,

representing the milestones in the progress of Irish literature from *Gulliver's Travels* to *Dracula, The Importance of Being Earnest, Ulysses* and *Waiting for Godot*. Most of these are first or early editions, recapturing the moment when they first surprised the world. There are books inscribed to Oliver Gogarty by W.B. Yeats and to Brinsley MacNamara by James Joyce, while a first edition of Patrick Kavanagh's *The Great Hunger* includes in the poet's own hand a stanza which the prudish publisher declined to print.

Portraits of Irish writers are everywhere, including fine originals by artists such as Edward McGuire, Harry Kernoff, Patrick Swift and Micheal Farrell. Among the many letters are an abject note from Sheridan to a creditor, a signed refusal from Bernard Shaw to provide an autograph, a letter from Yeats to Frank O'Connor, a typically concise card from Samuel Beckett and Brendan Behan's postcard from Los Angeles ("Great spot for a quiet piss-up").

Among the pens, pipes and typewriters there are some particularly curious personal possessions — Lady Gregory's lorgnette, Austin Clarke's desk, Samuel Beckett's telephone, Mary Lavin's teddy bear, Oliver Gogarty's laurels and Brendan Behan's union card, complete with fingerprints — and such exotic intrusions as Handel's chair and a silver tazza decorated with scenes from the work of Burns.

Dublinia and the Viking World

Contact Information

St Michael's Hill
Christchurch, Dublin 8
Tel: 01 6794611
Email: info@dublinia.ie
Web: www.dublinia.ie

Opening Hours

April to September, daily,
10.00 to 5.00
October to March, Monday to Friday,
11.00 to 4.00; Sundays, 10.00 to 4.00
Admission fees: Adult, €6.00;
Children, €3.75; Family, €16.00

Facilities

Café (April to August)
Bookshop
Wheelchair access

How to Find Us

Located near Christchurch Cathedral
in Dublin city centre.

Dublinia and The Viking World exhibitions are owned and operated by the Medieval Trust, a charitable trust established to increase knowledge and understanding of the medieval period. The exhibitions are housed in the former Synod Hall, adjacent to Christ Church Cathedral. This beautiful neo-Gothic building was completed in 1875, around the same time as the restoration of Christ Church Cathedral, under the direction of the Victorian architect, G.E. Street. The Medieval Trust funds the ongoing conservation of this beautiful landmark building.

Dublinia and The Viking World are complementary exhibitions which bring to life two of the most vibrant periods of Irish history. As part of the Trust's aim to bring a wider knowledge of history, the exhibitions are engaging, accessible and designed to spark your interest in finding out more about these fascinating times.

Dublinia traces the history of Dublin from the arrival of Strongbow and his knights to Dublin in 1170 up to the burning of the monasteries under Henry VIII in 1540. The Viking World explores the story of the Vikings from their origins in Scandinavia, tracing their extraordinary rise to dominance in Western Europe. Using a combination of audio/visual, reconstruction and graphics, the exhibitions bring the past vividly to life in an accessible and entertaining way. Superbly researched and beautifully presented, there is something here for everyone from children to adults. A reasonable admission fee with the option of a discounted admission to Christ Church Cathedral (the buildings are linked by an elegant covered bridge), allow visitors to spend an enjoyable, informative afternoon at the heart of old Dublin and support the ongoing preservation work of the Medieval Trust.

Highlights from the Collection

Highlights include the reconstructed face of a medieval woman, generated from a medieval skeleton found at the edge of the River Liffey. Using contemporary reconstructive techniques, scientists have allowed us to see our medieval ancestor exactly as she would have looked. During the high season, Viking and medieval characters populate the exhibitions, demonstrating crafts and skills and telling tales of battles and seafaring. Check website or telephone for details.

Educational Programmes

Dublinia and The Viking World offer an extensive education programme for schools, adult learning and special interest groups. Activities include guided tours of the exhibitions, "Dig" workshops, medieval and Viking walking tours and the "Viking in the Classroom" project. A teacher's Resource Pack is provided to all pre-booked groups free of charge. A small library is available to primary and secondary level students for project work; access is by appointment only. For further details, please contact our Education Officer.

Dublin's City Hall —
The Story of the Capital

Contact Information

City Hall, Dame Street
Dublin 2
Tel: 01 2222204
Email: cityhall@dublincity.ie
Web: www.dublincity.ie

Opening Hours

Monday to Saturday, 10.00 to 5.15
Sunday, 2.00 to 5.00
Admission fees: **Adult,** €4.00;
Seniors and Unwaged, €1.50,
Children, €1.50

Facilities

Restaurant
Gift shop
Wheelchair access

How to Find Us

Located in Dublin's city centre, near
Christchurch and Temple Bar, just
outside the gates of Dublin Castle.

The Story of the Capital in Dublin's City Hall is an exciting multimedia exhibition tracing the history of Dublin City. It tells of the city's founding, from Viking times, through prosperity and oppression, into the unique and vibrant city of today. Treasures of the city, from the original city seal to the chains of the Lord Mayor, are on display, together with medieval manuscripts, period costumes and contemporary art. Newsreel clips and interactive screens offer a fascinating insight into the city's evolution.

City Hall itself is a spectacular piece of architecture, designed by Thomas Cooley and built as the Royal Exchange for a then prosperous Dublin merchant population between 1769 and 1779. Dublin City Council has owned the building since 1851 and has recently restored it to its original beauty.

*The Story of the Capital
Exhibition at City Hall*

City Hall played a part in the development of Irish nationalism. The funerals of leading Irish patriots,

City Hall building from Parliament Street

Charles Stewart Parnell and Jeremiah O'Donovan Rossa, were held from there and City Hall was garrisoned by the insurgents during the Easter Rising of 1916. In 1922, City Hall became the temporary headquarters of the Irish Provisional Government under its Chairman Michael Collins. The funerals of Collins, and of his colleague Arthur Griffith, both later took place from City Hall.

Highlights from the Collection

The exhibition's highlights include the original Lord Mayors' Chain and the Great City Sword and Mace.

The building itself must be one of the major highlights of any visit. City Hall is an outstanding example of the Georgian architecture for which

Dublin is world famous. It was built between 1769 and 1779 by the Guild of Merchants as the Royal Exchange, at a cost of £58,000, most of which was raised by public lotteries. The architect was Thomas Cooley, winner of a competition to design the building, with his more illustrious contemporary James Gandon in second place. The Royal Exchange belonged to the first rank of European architecture and marked the introduction to Ireland of the neo-classical style then fashionable on the Continent. The circular hall, or Rotunda, which was surmounted by a spacious dome supported by twelve columns was surrounded by an ambulatory where the merchants could stroll and discuss business. The sheer size and sumptuous fittings of the Exchange, with carved capitals by Simon Vierpyl and plasterwork by the leading stuccodore Charles Thorp, reflect

The history of the city is explained in interesting and exciting ways

the standing and prestige of Dublin in the eighteenth century.

Educational/Special Programmes

Free tours of the building are available to schools/colleges and other groups visiting the exhibition on request.

The gilded ceiling of the Rotunda at City Hall

Fry Model Railway

Contact Information

Malahide Castle Demesne
Malahide, Co Dublin
Tel: 01 846 3779
Email: fryrailway@dublintourism.ie
Web: www.visitdublin.com

Opening Hours

April to September, Monday to Saturday (closed Friday), 10.00 to 5.00 (closed 1.00 to 2.00)
Sundays and holidays, 2.00 to 6.00
Admission fees: **Adult**, €6.70; Children, €4.20; Family, €19.00

Facilities

Restaurant
Gift shop
Wheelchair access

How to Find Us

Located in the grounds of Malahide Castle.

The Fry Model Railway Museum is a unique collection of rare handmade models of more than 300 Irish trains, from the introduction of rail to the present.

Situated in the grounds surrounding Malahide Castle, this collection is a treat for railway enthusiasts, children and adults alike. One of the world's largest miniature railways, the exhibition is unique in that it is a working railway covering an area of 2,500 square feet.

The beautifully engineered models are from a collection originally built up in the 1920s and 1930s by Cyril Fry, a railway engineer and draughtsman, each piece assembled with the finest attention to detail. Irish and international exhibits from the earliest railway developments are run on a Grand Transport Complex which includes stations, bridges, trams, barges and even the River Liffey.

An exhibit at the Fry Model Railway Museum

The GAA Museum

Contact Information

St Joseph's Avenue
Croke Park, Dublin 3
Tel: 01 8192323
Email: gaamuseum@crokepark.ie
Web: www.gaa.ie/museum

Opening Hours

Open daily, Monday to Saturday,
9.30 to 6.00; Sunday, 12.00 to 5.00
Admission: Adults €5.50; Children,
€3.50; Students, €4.00; Family, €15.00

Facilities

Café
Gift shop
Wheelchair access

How to Find Us

Located in the Cusack Stand, via St.
Joseph's Avenue off Clonliffe Road.

The GAA Museum was established to commemorate, recognise and celebrate the GAA's contribution to Irish sporting, cultural and social life since its foundation in 1884. The museum, which is located in Croke Park and opened in 1998, looks at the birth and growth of the GAA at home and abroad, and its unique role in the national movement and cultural revival in Ireland.

Over 40 audio-visual presentations bring to life the players, matches, unique moments and countless memories of the past. Film presentations include topics such as the GAA's role in thte struggle for independence and the excitement of All-Ireland Final Day. Touchscreen technology enables the visitor to instantly recall historic moments, great players and great games. Specially designed interactives allow visitors to test their own skills in hurling and Gaelic football.

The museum's permanant exhibition, which extends to two floors, is self-guided and fully accessible for visitors with special needs. Also available are guided tours of Croke Park which offer an in-depth, behind the scenes look at one of the most historic and modern sporting arenas in the world.

Highlights from the Collection

Highlights include the medal collections of Jack Lynch, Christy Ring, Noel Skehan and others; the Sam Maguire Cup and the Liam MacCarthy Cup; and the 20-minute

Ground floor of museum interior

audiovisual show *National Awakening*, which examines GAA members' roles in the achievement of national independence.

Special Programmes

In 2005 the GAA Museum initiated a programme of special events, such as story-telling and a hurley-making demonstration which took place at weekends. This programme will be developed further in 2006.

"There is no such thing as inaccuracy in a photograph. All photographs are accurate. None of them is the truth."

— Richard Avedon

Gallery of Photography

Contact Information

Meeting House Square
Temple Bar, Dublin 2
Tel: 01 6714654
Email: gallery@irish-photography.com
Web: www.irish-photography.com

Opening Hours

Tuesday to Saturday, 11.00 to 6.00
Sunday 1.00 to 6.00
No admission fee

Facilities

Gift shop
Wheelchair access

How to Find Us

Located between Eustace Street and
Sycamore Street in Temple Bar.

Since its inception in 1978 the Gallery of Photography has become Ireland's premier venue for photography. The gallery, which has staged exhibitions with many of the major names in contemporary photography, moved to its new location, a purpose-built space with fully fitted darkrooms, in Meeting House Square in 1995.

Some of the gallery's activities include hosting exhibitions, running photography courses and workshops, and providing darkroom facilities for hire.

The gallery bookshop stocks Ireland's widest range of photographic publications. As well as popularly priced books, our range includes hard to find editions, lomo cameras

A public event at the Gallery of Photography

and a huge selection of unusual postcards.

The gallery, which is non-profit-making, is funded by the Arts Council and Dublin Corporation.

Inside the Gallery of Photography

Ireland's Historic Science Centre

Contact Information

Birr Castle Demesne
Birr, Co. Offaly
Tel: 0509 20336
Email: mail@birrcastle.com
Web: www.birrcastle.com

Opening Hours

Open daily 17 March to October,
9.00 to 6.00; rest of year, 10.00 to 4.00
Admission fees: **Adult,** €9.00;
Students/Seniors, €7.00; Children,
€5.00

Facilities

Restaurant
Gift shop
Wheelchair access

How to Find Us

Located in the centre of Birr in the
Birr Castle Demesne.

Ireland's Historic Science Centre in Birr Castle Demesne is almost certainly unique. Worldwide it is unlikely that there is another which can demonstrate the same consistency of scientific, technological and artistic achievement over four generations of the same family embracing astronomy, engineering, photography, botany/horticulture.

The intention of the Centre is to demonstrate in the most positive way possible that the whole island of Ireland has made a most distinguished contribution to the history of science and technology worldwide. This is in contrapuntal distinction to the prevailing impression shared by people both inside and outside Ireland that Ireland's cultural history is based almost exclusively in the literary and musical art forms.

The current galleries concentrate on the achievements of those scientists and engineers most closely associated with Birr over the past 200 years. Their achievements are displayed in the context of their most modern application. Sir Charles

Engineerium

Parsons' Steam Turbine is not only notable for the role it played in the late nineteenth and early twentieth century British navy, but continues to have immediate significance in the basic formula for all turbo jet air travel and similar power items in the production of electricity.

Each gallery contains items most of which are actually at home in Birr. The most striking illustration of this is the Lunar Heat Machine designed by the Fourth Earl of Rosse to measure the heat of the moon from the earth. This machine represents in elegant simplicity the imaginative genius of mind that characterises so many of the pioneering scientific and technological inventions associated with the Parsons family.

Because of the importance of demonstrating at the outset of the

Universal Joint

twenty-first century that women have a coequal ability with men to contribute outstanding achievements to the enterprises of science and technology, great emphasis has been laid on the contribution of Mary Countess of Rosse to the development of photography in the 1840s; of Mary Ward (her cousin by marriage) to microscopy in the same period; and to Anne Countess of Rosse to garden and landscape design in the second half of the twentieth century.

The centre is set in a demesne which itself is a living, evolving landscape of engineering, scientific and horticultural endeavour. Engineering is represented in the 1822 suspension bridge, the water works feeding the lake and the Turbine house. The Leviathan telescope, for 70 years the largest in the world, demonstrates both science and technology.

Educational Programmes

Conscious of nationwide declining numbers of science students at university level, the centre has developed two programmes aimed at both the Primary and Junior Science Curriculum. These programmes provide practical activities with an experience of the adventure of scientific discovery outside the classroom.

The Discovery Primary Science is a fun cartoon programme that en-

The Leviathan Telescope

courages children to explore their surroundings and ask questions of the most obvious – why do stars twinkle and why do leaves fall off trees each year?

The Junior Science Trail combines a botany field trip to the award-winning gardens with an interactive museum visit. Student activities cover curriculum areas in chemistry, physics and biology such as light, energy conversion, living things, ecology and classification of substances.

Additional Comments

Ireland's Historic Science Centre received the Gulbenkian/Heritage Centre Small Museum of the Year Award 2002.

"History is a guide to
navigation in perilous times.
History is who we are and why
we are the way we are."

— David C. McCullough

Irish Agricultural Museum

Contact Information

Johnstown Castle Estate
Wexford
Tel: 053 42888

Opening Hours

June to August, Monday to Friday,
9.00 to 5.00; Saturday, Sunday, 11.00
to 5.00. April to May and September
to November, Monday to Friday,
9.00 to 12.30 and 1.30 to 5.00;
Saturday and Sunday, 2.00 to 5.00.
November to March, Monday to
Friday, 9.00 to 12.30 and 1.30 to 5.00;
closed Saturday and Sunday

Admission fees: **Adult,** €6.00;
Children, €4.00; Family, €20.00

Facilities

Café (summer only)
Gift shop
Wheelchair access

How to Find Us

Located 6 km southwest of Wexford
town on road to Kilmore Quay via
Murrintown.

This award-winning museum, which opened 30 years ago, has 30,000 square feet of display area supported by a library, archive, workshop, seasonal café and storage. The subjects of agriculture and rural life are dealt with in themed displays like the dairy, the laundry, the country kitchen, horse transport, the beet crop, the rural trades and so on. The history of the potato and of the great Irish famine (1845–48) is the subject of a special exhibition considered to be one of the best in Ireland.

Replica of mid-nineteenth-century Labourer's House in Famine Exhibition

Highlights from the Collection

Highlights include extensive displays on rural transport, farming and the activities of the farmyard and the farmhouse; an important collection of Irish country furniture with over 100 pieces; and large-scale replicas

Ferguson System Exhibition

of the workshops of the blacksmith, cooper, wheelwright, harness maker and basket maker. There are also displays on the Ferguson system and gardening.

New Developments

A new section will be completed for 2006 that presents three correctly furnished kitchens typical of farmhouses from the years 1800, 1900 and 1950. The newly established Ferguson System exhibition is also being extended for 2006.

Educational Programmes

The museum promotes pre-planned visits by school groups of 25 or less.

Additional Comments

Johnstown Castle is surrounded by 50 acres of ornamental gardens, which include three lakes, a medieval tower house, walled gardens with hothouses and over 200 species of mature trees and shrubs. A car-free zone with many different walks, all on level ground, and a serviced picnic area are also on the grounds. Peacocks wander free. The Irish Agricultural Museum is within the gardens.

Irish Fly Fishing and Game Shooting Museum

Contact Information

Attana House, Attanagh
Portlaoise, Co. Laois
Tel: 0502 36112
Email: info@irishfishingandhunting museum.com
Web: www.irishfishingandhunting museum.com

Opening Hours

Open daily all year from 10.00 to 6.00
Admission: Adults €5.00; Children, €2.00

Facilities

Gift shop

How to Find Us

Located five minutes off the main Dublin–Cork road, N8, between Abbeyleix and Durrow.

The Irish Fly Fishing and Game Shooting Museum is housed in an old farmhouse in Attanagh, a quaint village in County Laois, and has a collection of over 5,000 artefacts. It is the only museum of its kind in Ireland presenting and

Sign outside the museum

interpreting fishing and shooting and country life activities. It provides a history of the rich heritage of the Irish countryside.

The aim of the museum is to collect, preserve, exhibit and interpret the equipment and tactics of fishing and shooting.

The first room is dedicated to the classic salmon flies. Then there is the library, a room dedicated to Gar-

netts and Keegans of Dublin, one of the biggest fishing and hunting shops in Ireland in its day. Another room is full of fly fishing and shooting memorabilia and there is also a trophy room full of game birds and animals.

There is a replica of a gunsmith's workshop from bygone days and there is also a gamekeeper's room full of traps. Finally there is a boat room and a hatching room.

Future Developments

There are plans to add on two more rooms, one for an Irish Fishing and Hunting Hall of Fame, and another devoted to the history and achievements of Irish gundogs.

An exhibit in the museum

Why Museums?

"Museums are the homes of objects of the past, reminding us where we came from, our traditions, cultures, hobbies and so on. We cannot proceed into the future without understanding the past. Museums help us to make the right decisions, and to make our world a better place so that we can live in harmony with one another."

— Walter Phelan, Owner,
Irish Fly Fishing and Game Shooting Museum

Irish Jewish Museum

Contact Information

3 Walworth Road, off Victoria Street
South Circular Road
Portobello, Dublin 8
Tel: 01 4901857 or 4531797

Opening Hours

May to September, Sunday, Tuesday
and Thursday, 11.30 to 3.30
October and April, Sunday only,
10.30 to 2.30.
Admission is free; donations are
appreciated

Facilities

Gift shop
Wheelchair access

How to Find Us

Located off South Circular Road near
the Grand Canal in Dublin 8.

The Irish-Jewish Museum is located in a former synagogue building with all its original features. The display includes memorabilia relating to the Jewish communities in Ireland, depicting their important, though small, place in Ireland's cultural and historical heritage.

The collection includes photographs, paintings, certificates, books, letters and artefacts concerning all aspects of Jewish life. The display covers 150 years of professional, commercial and artistic activities and includes a gallery with Jewish religious objects. The original kitchen in the building recreates a typical sabbath meal setting of the early 1900s. The museum was opened in 1985 by Irish-born President Chaim Herzog of Israel.

Ark covers from former synagogues

The museum is divided into several areas and the synagogue portion presents a unique picture of the old type of small synagogue which dates from the early 1900s.

New Developments/Future Plans

The goal of the museum is to expand by incorporating three adjoining buildings. However this project will depend on the availability of funding from generous donors.

Educational/Special Programmes

The outreach programme of the museum is directed at tourists, adult, special interest and school groups. Talks and guided tours are provided to meet the needs of each particular group. Prior booking is essential to ensure facilities can be provided.

Ark with Torah scrolls

"Most painting in the European
tradition was painting the mask.
Modern art rejected all that.
Our subject matter was the
person behind the mask."

— Robert Motherwell

Irish Museum of Modern Art

Contact Information

Royal Hospital, Military Road
Kilmainham, Dublin 8
Tel: 01 6129900
Email: info@imma.ie
Web: www.imma.ie

Opening Hours

Tuesday to Saturday, 10.00 to 5.30
(except Wednesday, 10.30 to 5.00)
Sunday, 12.00 to 5.30; closed Monday
No admission fee

Facilities

Café
Bookshop
Wheelchair access

How to Find Us

Museum entrance is on
Military Road, five minutes' walk
from Heuston Station.

The Irish Museum of Modern Art was established by the Government in 1990 as Ireland's first national institution for the presentation and collection of modern and contemporary art, and was officially opened by the then Taoiseach, Charles Haughey, on 25 May 1991. The museum presents a wide variety of art in a dynamic programme of exhibitions, which regularly includes bodies of work from its own collection and its award-winning Education and Community Department. It also creates more widespread access to art and artists through its Studio and National programmes.

Historic Building

All of IMMA's activities are greatly enhanced by the museum's magnificent building and grounds. The Royal Hospital Kilmainham, the finest 17th-century building in Ireland, was built in 1684 as a home for retired soldiers and continued in that use for almost 250 years. Its style is based

Irish Museum of Modern Art

on Les Invalides in Paris, with a formal facade and large elegant courtyard. The museum site also includes a formal garden, meadow and medieval burial grounds. Guided heritage tours of the Royal Hospital Kilmainham are available during the summer season. A permanent heritage exhibition and video are on view all year round.

Highlights from the Collection

The museum's collection, which comprises more than 4,300 works, has been developed since 1990 through purchase, donations and long-term loans, as well as by the occasional commissioning of new works. IMMA purchases contemporary art but accepts donations and loans of more historical art objects, with particular emphasis on work from the 1940s onwards.

The permanent collection reflects some of the most exciting trends in Irish and international art, including paintings by Francesco Clemente, Louis le Brocquy, Michael Craig-Martin, Tony O'Malley and Paula Rego; sculptures by Damien Hirst, Antony Gormley and Dorothy Cross; installations by Rebecca Horn, Joseph Kosuth and Ann Hamilton; filmworks by Gillian Wearing, Clare Langan and Jaki Irvine, and photoworks by Thomas Ruff, Gilbert and George and Willie Doherty. Major donations include a wide variety of modern and contemporary art, including a number of 1930s works by Picasso, paintings by Sean Scully, a large sculpture by Barry Flanagan and a film by Neil Jordan. Loans to the collection include an important body of work by outsider, or self-taught, artists in the Musgrave Kinley Outsider Collection.

On average four or five exhibitions drawn from the collection are shown at the museum each year, comprising large-scale exhibitions in the West Wing First Floor Galleries and smaller, often themed, shows in the Ground Floor Galleries. Exhibitions from the collection have toured increasingly in recent years, including to Boston, Philadelphia, Chicago and Virginia in the USA, to St John's, Newfoundland in Canada and to Beijing and Shanghai in China.

Gary Hume, "Back of Snowman", 2003

Exhibitions

The museum's temporary exhibitions programme, presenting up to

Sean Scully, 7/7/91 in Memory of Robyn Walker, *1991*

12 separate exhibitions each year, frequently juxtaposes the work of well-established figures with that of younger generation artists to create a debate about the nature and function of art. Exhibitions by leading international artists, many being shown for the first time in Ireland, are staged on a regular basis. This has included such internationally acclaimed artists as Jasper Johns, Laurie Anderson, Sophie Calle and Marc Quinn, together with rapidly rising names like Fred Tomaselli, Mark Manders and Pierre Huyghe. Irish artists are also strongly represented, as in the Dorothy Cross survey show, the Tony O'Malley retrospective and an exhibition from the Contemporary Irish Art Society. IMMA originates many of its exhibitions but also works closely with a wide network of international museums and galleries.

New Developments/Future Plans

Starting in 2006, IMMA is embarking on a change in the nature and scale of its temporary exhibition programme. This will involve a number of exhibitions by eminent international artists, such as Howard Hodgkin, Michael Craig-Martin and Barry Flanagan in 2006; Georgia O'Keeffe and Lucien Freud in 2007; and James Coleman in 2008. These exhibitions would aim to be definitive of their type and would tour to a number of prestigious museums and galleries abroad. A number of shows by leading younger-generation artists, involving specially commissioned works and performance pieces, are also planned.

In autumn 2006 IMMA is organising a high-profile international symposium on creating access to contemporary art modelled on the successful symposium on curating staged in 2004. In addition to creating a forum for the discussions of best practice in this important area, the symposium will also serve to highlight IMMA's standing as a leader in the field of education and community programming.

Education and Community Programmes

An extensive range of programmes has been developed by the museum's Education and Community Department with the intention of creating and increasing access to the visual arts, as well as engagement with their meaning and practice. The programmes operate on many levels — with research projects in association with the Department of Education and Science, with community initiatives within the local catchment area and with the general public in

Community programme at IMMA

the gallery-based Explorer family programme on Sundays.

A number of programmes have been put in place for groups who wish to have contact with specific exhibitions or artists, including gallery discussions and practical studio work. The ongoing primary school programme creates access for individual teachers, staff groups and children.

A wide variety of talks and lectures by artists and curators, available to the general public, are organised each year.

The James Joyce Museum

Contact Information

Joyce Tower
Sandycove, Co. Dublin
Tel: 01 2809265
Email: joycetower@dublintourism.ie
Web: www.visitdublin.com

Opening Hours

Open March to October,
Monday to Saturday, 10.00 to 5.00;
Sunday, 2.00 to 6.00
Admission fees: **Adult**, €6.70;
Children, €4.20; Family, €19.00

How to Find Us

Located eight miles south of Dublin
city centre and one mile from Dun
Laoghaire along the coast road.

Like the many other Martello towers around Dublin, the Joyce Tower was built in 1804 to withstand a threatened invasion by Napoleon. The French never arrived, and a hundred years later the British War Department put the tower up for rent. The first tenant was the poet Oliver St John Gogarty, who moved in in August 1904 and invited his friend James Joyce to stay. By the time Joyce took up the invitation in early September he had spoiled his welcome by insulting Gogarty (and most of the other Irish writers) in a poem called "The Holy Office". Gogarty, wary of further such attacks, honoured the invitation, but relations deteriorated and

after less than a week Joyce had to depart in a hurry when Gogarty fired a gun over his head in the middle of the night. He left Ireland altogether a month later.

Joyce duly got his revenge with the publication in 1922 of *Ulysses*. The opening of the book was set in the Tower and implied that Joyce was the one who had paid the rent – much to the annoyance of Gogarty, who had played host there for several years. The building, which was sold in 1922, inevitably became famous as "James Joyce's Tower" and began to attract literary pilgrims. It was acquired in 1954 by the architect Michael Scott, who lived next door, and he and his friends set up the Joyce Tower Society to establish a James Joyce Museum there. A collection began to come together, and a generous financial contribution by the film-maker John Huston finally got the museum opened on Bloomsday, 16 June 1962, when Sylvia Beach, the original publisher of *Ulysses*, came from Paris to raise the flag over the Tower.

Objects in the museum bring Joyce and his works vividly to life. The collection includes letters, photographs, portraits and personal possessions, some of them given by close friends such as Samuel Beckett, Maria Jolas, Sylvia Beach and Paul Ruggiero – his tie and wallet, his cabin trunk, guitar and cane are among these. There are first and rare editions of his work, including his early broadsides and the celebrated edition of *Ulysses* illustrated by Henri Matisse. Items such as the original key of the Tower, a Clongowes pandybat, a Plumtree's pot and photographs of "Throwaway" and Davy Stephens are examples of the real and ordinary which Joyce transformed into the material of myth.

Locke's Distillery Museum

Contact Information

Kilbeggan
Co. Westmeath
Tel: 057 9332134
Email: lockesmuseum@iol.ie
Web: www.lockesdistillerymuseum.com

Opening Hours

April to October, daily, 9.00 to 6.00; November to March, daily, 10.00 to 4.00
Admission fees: **Adult**, €5.50; Students/Seniors, €4.75
Family, €12.00

Facilities

Restaurant
Gift shop
Wheelchair access

How to Find Us

Located on the main street in Kilbeggan town, on the N6 Dublin to Galway road.

At the Locke's Distillery Museum visitors can take a step back in time and visit the "oldest licensed pot still distillery in the world", established in 1757. Guided tours go through the old distillery buildings where most of the original machinery, which has been restored, can be seen working daily.

Visitors can follow the process from the grinding of the grain to the casking of the final product; see the restored 1887 steam engine and watch the nieneteenth-century waterwheel drive the machinery; peer into the nine-metre high fermentation vats; watch as the cooper tightens the hoops on the aged barrels; and stroll through the bonded warehouse and let the aroma of maturing whiskey arouse their senses. They can also learn about the lives and working conditions of the people who worked here. The exhibition houses many whiskey-related artefacts and has a children's play area.

The tour ends in the tasting bar with a complimentary glass of Kilbeggan Irish Whiskey.

*Water Wheel at Locke's
Distillery Museum*

Steam Powered Beam Engine

Malahide Castle

Contact Information

Malahide
Co. Dublin
Tel: 01 8462184
Web: www.malahidecastle.com

Opening Hours

April to September, Monday to Saturday, 10.00 to 5.00, Sundays and Public Holidays, 10.00 to 6.00 October to March, Monday to Saturday, 10.00 to 5.00, Sunday and Public Holidays, 11.00 to 5.00. Closed for tours 12.45 to 2.00.

Admission fees: **Adult**, €6.70; Children, €4.20; Family, €19.00

Facilities

Restaurant
Gift shop
Wheelchair access

How to Find Us

Located just outside the village of Malahide.

Malahide Castle, set on 250 acres of park land in the pretty seaside town of Malahide, was both a fortress and a private home for nearly 800 years. The Talbot family lived here from 1185 to 1973, when the last Lord Talbot died.

The house is furnished with beautiful period furniture together with an extensive collection of Irish portrait paintings, mainly from the National Gallery. The history of the Talbot family is recorded in the Great Hall, with portraits of generations of the family telling their own story of Ireland's stormy history. One of the more poignant legends concerns the morning of the Battle of the Boyne in 1690, when 14 members of the family breakfasted together in this room, never to return, as all were dead by nightfall.

At the heart of the medieval castle is the Oak Room, approached by a winding stone staircase and lit by Gothic windows added in 1820 when the room was enlarged and the front hall below was created. The room is lined with carved oak from floor to ceiling, representing scriptural subjects, now black with age and polishing. Some of the carving is of Flemish origin, including six panels representing biblical scenes opposite the window; their religious theme suggests that the Talbots, who remained Roman Catholics until 1774, used this room as a chapel in penal times. Over the mantelpiece is a fine representation of the coronation of the Blessed Virgin which, according to tradition disappeared when Cromwell seized the Castle and miraculously sprang back to its place when the Talbots were reinstated.

Inside Malahide Castle

National Gallery of Ireland

Contact Information

Merrion Square West and
Clare Street, Dublin 2
Tel: 01 6615133
Email: info@ngi.ie
Web: www.nationalgallery.ie

Opening Hours

Monday to Saturday, 9.30 to 5.50
Thursday, 9.30 to 8.30
Sunday, 12.00 to 5.30.
Admission is free.

Facilities

Restaurant
Gift shop
Wheelchair acceess

How to find us

Located in the city centre across from
Merrion Square.

The National Gallery of Ireland was founded by an Act of Parliament in 1854 and opened its doors to the public in 1864. The gallery has been extended over the years to accomodate its growing collection. In January 2002 the gallery opened a 4,000 square metre extension named the Millennium Wing which accommodates enhanced exhibition space and visitor facilities.

Permanent Collection

The National Gallery of Ireland houses 13,000 works of art which comprise the most important and representative collection of Irish art (seventeenth to twentieth centuries) and all the major schools of Western European art (thirteenth to twentieth centuries). Highlights of the collec-

Winter Garden at the National Gallery

Jules Breton (1827–1906) The Gleaners: Courrieres, Pas de Calais, *1854*

tion include European masterpieces by Fra Angelico, Mantegna, Caravaggio, Titian, Poussin, Rembrandt, Vermeer, El Greco, Goya, Van Dyck, Gainsborough and Reynolds.

Among the Irish artists represented are Thomas Roberts, Hugh Douglas Hamilton, James Barry, James A. Connor, Nathaniel Hone, Walter Osborne, Roderic Connor, William Orpen, John Lavery, Mainie Jellett, Paul Henry, Gerard Dillon and Louis le Brocquy. There is also a National Portrait Collection and a special room devoted to the artistic works of Ireland's most celebrated twentieth-century artist Jack B. Yeats and members of his family.

Programmes and Services

The Gallery runs an extensive public programme of tours, talks, special exhibitions and a wide range of education activities for all ages. Free guided tours of the collection meet in the Shaw Room on Saturdays at

3.00 pm and on Sundays at 2.00 pm, 3.00 pm and 4.00 pm. Public talks take place in the Lecture Theatre on Tuesdays at 10.30 am and Sunday at 3.00 pm (free). Family packs are available from the information desks, and a family programme runs every Saturday at 3.00 pm (except July, August and December). Children's talks, school programmes, art studies and drawing study courses are also part of the annual programme.

George Barret (1732–1784) View of Powerscourt Waterfall, Co. Wicklow

Research Services

The National Gallery of Ireland Fine Art Library collection comprises over 50,000 publications relating to art from the fifteenth century to the present day. There is a particular focus on painting, prints and drawings, but sculpture and architecture are also well represented. The Library is open to members of the public by appointment.

ESB Centre for the Study of Irish Art

The Centre for the Study of Irish Art houses archive material relevant to the study of Irish art. Selected highlights include primary material relating to individual artists, groups and institutions from the eighteenth century to the present day. ARTseARCH, the gallery's digital archive system, provides access to items from the gallery's archive collection. The Centre is open to members of the public by appointment.

Diageo Print Room

The Print Room provides researchers and the general public with supervised access to the Gallery's wide-ranging collection of prints and drawings. Highlights include Irish and British landscapes and old master drawings from the Italian, French and Dutch schools. Open to members of the public by appointment.

Yeats Archive

The Yeats Archive houses a prestigious collection of material relating to Jack B. Yeats and members of the Yeats family. Open to members of the public by appointment.

"A country that has few
museums is both materially
poor and spiritually poor. . . .
Museums, like theatres and
libraries, are a means to freedom."

— Sister Wendy Beckett

National Museum of Ireland
Archaeology and History

Contact Information

Kildare Street
Dublin 2
Tel: 01 6777444
Email: marketing@museum.ie
Web: www.museum.ie

Opening Hours

Tuesday to Saturday, 10.00 to 5.00
Sunday, 2.00 to 5.00
Admission is free.

Facilities

Café
Gift shop
Wheelchair access (ground floor)

How to Find Us

Located on Kildare Street, beside Dáil
Éireann.

The National Museum of Ireland Archaeology and History is the national repository for all archaeological objects found in Ireland. This museum houses over 2,000,000 artefacts which range in date between 7,000 BC and the late medieval period.

Exhibitions include the finest collection of prehistoric gold artefacts in western Europe, outstanding examples of metalwork from the Celtic Iron Age, as well as the museum's world-renowned collection of medieval ecclesiastical objects and jewellery. The Broighter Hoard, the Ardagh Chalice, the Tara Brooch and Derrynaflan Hoard are among the masterpieces on display. The museum also houses a rich collection of Egyptian material.

The National Museum of Ireland, Kildare Street officially opened its

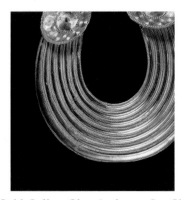

Gold Collar, Gleeninsheen, Co. Clare

doors to the public in August 1890. The building was designed by Thomas Newenham Deane and his son Thomas Manly Deane and has been described as "an accomplished exercise in Victorian Palladianism". The rotunda or entrance hall is 18 me-

tres high and is decorated with classical columns of Irish marble. The rotunda opens onto a great central court and gallery. Exhibition rooms

Egyptian Mummy

are located around the court on the ground floor and off the gallery on the first floor.

The mosaic floors are decorated with scenes from classical mythology and allegory and were laid by Ludwig Oppenheimer of Manchester. The intricate door panels feature a wealth of motifs and were carved by Carlo Cambi of Siena while the door architraves, executed in blue, yellow and white majolica, were manufactured by Burmantofts of Leeds.

The museum is home to the Irish Antiquities Division, which is responsible for the portable archaeological heritage of Ireland. In addition to managing the archaeological collections the staff are also charged with caring for the substantial Ethnographical, Classical and Egyptian collections.

National Museum of Ireland
Decorative Arts & History

Contact Information

Benburb Street
Dublin 7
Tel: 01 6777444
Email: marketing@museum.ie
Web: www.museum.ie

Opening Hours

Tuesday to Saturday, 10.00 to 5.00
Sunday, 2.00 to 5.00
Admission is free.

Facilities

Café
Gift shop
Wheelchair access

How to Find Us

Located at Collins Barracks, Benburb Street, one mile west of the City on the North Quays.

The Museum of Decorative Arts and History is home to a wide range of objects which include weaponry, furniture, silver, ceramics and glassware, as well as examples of folklife and costume. The exhibitions have been designed in innovative and contemporary galleries. The Fonthill Vase, a Chinese vase made about 1300 AD, is one of the rarest pieces in the Museum. It is world-renowned as one of the best documented pieces of early porcelain. The William Smith O'Brien Gold Cup, the Eileen Gray chrome table and the Lord Chancellor's Mace are also among the highlights.

The initial buildings at Collins Barracks were started in 1702 and were designed by Captain Thomas Burgh. The complex, which includes eighteenth and nineteenth century

Jupiter in Coral c.1830

buildings, housed troops continually for over three centuries. Originally the complex was known as "The Barracks", but changed in the early nineteenth century to the "Royal Barracks". In 1922 the whole com-

Skinners alley armchair, carved giltwood c. 1730

plex was handed over to the troops of the Free State army and was immediately named Collins Barracks after Michael Collins, the first commander-in-chief of the Irish Free State.

In 1994, Collins Barracks was assigned to the National Museum of Ireland. The buildings were completely renovated and restored to become the Museum of Decorative Arts and History, which opened in September 1997. Three floors of exhibition galleries were refurbished on two of the wings of the best surviving square, Clarke Square. Over

2,500 square metres of space was devoted to the introductory exhibitions, outlining the museum's chequered history and showcasing some of the prime collections long hidden from public view.

Today, Collins Barracks is the administrative headquarters for the four branches that now constitute the National Museum of Ireland. Since the first phase of exhibitions was formally opened, additional galleries have been added. These include the Riding School, which accommodates temporary exhibitions and a state-of-the-art conservation laboratory has also been opened on the western side of the site. When the large second-phase building is completed at Collins Barracks it will accommodate additional historical exhibitions and permanent galleries for both the Ethnographical and Earth Science collections.

The Museum of Decorative Arts and History is home to the Art and Industrial Division of the National Museum of Ireland. The Division is responsible for over a quarter of a million artefacts reflecting Irish economic, social, industrial, political and military history over the last three centuries. In addition to managing these collections, staff care for collections of Irish, European and Oriental decorative arts which give an understanding of international design and culture as they relate to Ireland.

Epergne

"There are some people who don't like museums because they think of them as tombs, or something negative. I've always loved them. They are to me lighthouses of utopianism and social well-being."

— *R.B. Kitaj*

National Museum of Ireland Natural History

Contact Information

Merrion Street
Dublin 2
Tel: 01 6777444
Email: marketing@museum.ie
Web: www.museum.ie

Opening Hours

Tuesday to Saturday, 10.00 to 5.00
Sunday, 2.00 to 5.00
Admission is free.

Facilities

Gift shop
Wheelchair access (limited)

How to Find Us

Located on Merrion Street next to the
National Gallery.

The National Museum of Ireland — Natural History, has approximately 10,000 animals on display which have been drawn from collections of over 2,000,000 specimens. These collections have been accumulating for over two centuries. Today this zoological museum encompasses outstanding examples of wildlife from Ireland and the far corners of the globe, some still to be seen today and others long extinct.

Just two years before Charles Darwin published his famous work on *The Origin of Species*, the Natural History Museum, Merrion Street was opened to the public for the first time, in 1857. This building was designed by Frederick V. Clarendon and is the oldest purpose-built museum building in Ireland, still used as originally intended. The museum is famous for its Victorian cabinet style, which houses "one of the world's finest and fullest collections", still to be seen today. The early origins of the museum lies with the Royal Dublin Society (RDS) which began gathering these collections in the eighteenth century. It was the enactment of The Dublin Science and Art Museum Act of 1877 which led to the transfer of the Natural History building and its collections to state ownership.

The National Museum of Ireland — Natural History is home to the Natural History Division which is responsible for caring for the museum collections in the disciplines

Toucan

of zoology and geology. In 2001 the Earth Science Section of the Division moved from rented accommodation to relocate to Collins Barracks where new offices, a library and archive rooms have been established. When the large second-phase building at Collins Barracks is completed it will house an Earth Science gallery dedicated to the geological collections of the Natural History Division. Information on the collections is available from the curators at naturalhistory@museum.ie and some collections catalogues are available online at www.ucd.ie/~zoology/museum.

Number Twenty Nine

Contact Information

29 Fitzwilliam Street Lower
Dublin 2
Tel: 01 7026165
Email numbertwentynine@esb.ie
Web: www.esbi.ie/numbertwentynine

Opening Hours

Tuesday to Saturday 10.00 to 5.00
Sunday 1.00 to 5.00.
Admission: Adults, €4.50, Concession
(Student, OAP, Unwaged), €2.00;
Children under 16 free.

Facilities

Café
Gift shop
Wheelchair acceess (partial)

How to find us

Located on Fitzwilliam Street Lower.
Entrance at junction of Fitzwilliam
Street Lower and Mount Street Up-
per, adjacent to Merrion Square.

Why Museums?

"Museums, because they are entrusted with the care of our material past and with that trust comes a responsibility to communicate all that makes our past unique.

Museums, because they present ourselves to ourselves.

In museums the objects do the talking. In the right hands, the objects have a lot to tell; of ordinary and extraordinary past lives. Some of these lives seem alien to us now. They seem to have been lived, quite literally, in another country; the unrecoverable past. Others are surprisingly familiar and close at hand. Sometimes there is nothing new under the sun.

Museums, because they are all this and more. We work in museums in the hope that, true to their name, they will inspire present and future generations."

— Kieran Burns, Curator,
Number Twenty Nine

Number Twenty Nine is Dublin's Georgian House Museum. This restored townhouse is located on Fitzwilliam Street Lower, adjacent to Merrion Square, in the heart of Dublin's Georgian quarter. Visitors take a guided tour from the basement to the attic, through rooms which have been furnished with original artefacts as they would have been in the years 1790 to 1820.

Number Twenty Nine was first occupied in 1794, during a time of great change and expansion in Ireland's capital. The first occupant was Mrs Olivia Beatty, the widow of a prominent Dublin wine merchant.

Much of the elegance of late Georgian Dublin, however, was superficial. Visiting the museum gives

The front hall at street level

fortunate who lived in such elegant townhouses, and the less fortunate who worked in them.

The museum captures life in the late eighteenth century and presents an insight into the social, cultural and political life of the capital.

Number Twenty Nine is a partnership between Electricity Supply Board and the National Museum of Ireland, and has been playing an important role since 1991 in making the history of late Georgian Dublin more accessible.

Highlights from the Collection

The museum contains an important collection of late Georgian furniture, art, ceramics, and glassware, illustrating middle class life in the late eighteenth and early nineteenth centuries.

Many fine cabinet makers worked in Dublin in the late Georgian period,

The pantry in the basement

young and old alike a chance to experience what life was like for the

such as William Moore and the nine-teenth-century firm of Mack, Williams and Gibton. Examples of work by both these makers can be seen in the house. Included in the exhibition is furniture from earlier in the eighteenth century, a time regarded by many as being the finest in the history of Irish furniture production. In the hallway of the house stands a long case clock, manufactured by John Sanderson, a second generation Huguenot refugee, whose father had fled religious insecurity in France. In the back drawing room are a number of examples of fine mid-eighteenth-century cabinet making.

The museum also houses an interesting and varied collection of prints, oil paintings, watercolours and sketches by well-known and lesser-known artists, including Thomas Roberts, Gilbert Stuart, G.F. Mulvany, Martin Archer Shee, William Saddler II and Nathaniel Hone. Also displayed are a number of paintings which are of particular interest to those interested in the history of Dublin city, such as an unusual view of Portobello in Rathmines by an English actor turned painter who came to Ireland initially to perform in the Smock Alley Theatre.

As important as any of the fine furniture or paintings are, equally interesting are the everyday artefacts and curiosities such as the cricket cage kept by the kitchen range to bring luck to the house; an early nineteenth-century exercise horse or liver shaker, designed by Thomas Sheraton to give a gentleman the ex-

The boudoir in the private quarters of the house

ercise he would normally get from horse riding, or the tiny oak baby walker used to train young children in taking their first steps.

New Developments/Future Plans

Number Twenty Nine is actively engaged in expanding its activities in education programming as well as its collection, through loans, donations, and purchasing, and to rotating displays with the National Museum of Ireland.

Educational/Special Programmes

The museum aims to communicate and interpret, among others aspects, the social, decorative, cultural and political history of the late Georgian capital. Its social, educational, and community outreach objectives stem from that remit, and the museum aims to make this exhibition as accessible and engaging as possible to as broad a cross-section of Irish and international audiences as can be achieved.

Number Twenty Nine regularly runs educational and outreach events such as themed guided tours, special educational workshops, lecture series, publications, and targeted group-based activities. The museum also facilitates research queries across a range of disciplines and levels. For details, see our website. The museum has also developed educational worksheets for primary and secondary students which can be downloaded from the website, as well as a CD and guide book of the house.

Portobello Harbour, circa 1809, to the south of Dublin city, by Thomas Snagg

The Pearse Museum

Contact Information

St Enda's Park
Rathfarnham, Dublin 16
Tel: 01 4934208

Opening Hours

Open daily, May to August, 10.00 to
5.30; September to October, 10.00 to
5.00; November to January, 10.00 to
4.00; February to April, 10.00 to 5.00
Admission is free

Facilities

Café (summer weekends only)
Wheelchair access

How to Find Us

Located on the Grange Road in Rathfarnham on the way to Marlay Park.

Twenty minutes from the city centre lies St. Enda's National Historic Park, the former home and school of Patrick and Willie Pearse. The brothers were executed for their part in the Easter Rising of 1916, the event that led ultimately to Ireland's polticial independence.

Patrick Pearse, writer and teacher, is one of the most important characters in modern Irish history. He brought

View of the Walled Garden from the House

his school, St. Enda's, to Rathfarnham in 1910. There he found an inspirational setting for his pioneering educational project. It now houses a museum which tells the story of his remarkable life.

Highlights from the Collection

Highlights include original documents and artefacts relating to the life of Patrick Pearse, including the

original draft of his oration at the graveside of O'Donovan Rossa. Also featured are original artefacts relating to his school, St. Enda's, and works by his brother Willie, as well as examples of the monumental sculpture of his father, James Pearse.

New Developments

The museum is scheduled to close in mid-2006 for a major refurbishment and new exhibitions and will re-open mid-2007.

Educational Programmes

The museum provides nature walks and other nature study activities through its Nature Study Centre for primary and secondary level children. The Nature Study Centre will remain open during the refurbishment period.

The Nature Study Centre

"Few people think more than two or three times a year. I have made an international reputation for myself by thinking once or twice a week."

— George Bernard Shaw

The Shaw Birthplace

Contact Information

33 Synge Street
Dublin 8
Tel: 01 4750854

Opening Hours

Open May to September, Monday to Friday, 10.00 to 1.00 and 2.00 to 5.00; closed all day Wednesday. Saturday, Sunday and Public Holidays, 2.00 to 5.00
Admission fees: **Adult,** €6.70; Children, €4.20; Family, €19.00

Facilities

Café (summer weekends only)
Wheelchair access

How to Find Us

Located on Synge Street, off the South Circular Road.

"Author of Many Plays" is the simple accolade to George Bernard Shaw on the plaque outside his birthplace and his Victorian home and early life mirrors this simplicity.

The first home of the Shaw family and the renowned playwright has been restored to its Victorian elegance and charm and has the appearance that the family have just gone out for the afternoon. The neat terraced house is as much a celebration of Victorian Dublin domestic life as of the early years of one of Dublin's Nobel Prize winners for literature.

It was in this house, opened to the public in 1993, that Shaw began to gather the store of characters who would later populate his books. From the drawing room where

Interior of Shaw Birthplace

Mrs. Shaw held many musical evenings, to the front parlour and children's bedrooms, this charming residence is a wonderful insight into the everyday life of Victorian Dublin.

Rooms on view are the kitchen, the maid's room, the nursery, the drawing room, and a couple of bedrooms, including young Bernard's.

The Shaw Birthplace

The Steam Museum

Contact Information

Lodge Park
Straffan, Co Kildare
Tel: 01 6273155
Email: info@steam-museum.ie
Web: www.steam-museum.ie

Opening Hours

Open June to August, Wednesday to Sunday, 2.00 to 6.00
May and September, open by appointment.
Admission: Adults €7.50; Concession, €5.00; Family, €20.00 (tech. and hort. students free of charge)

Facilities

Tea shop
Gift shop
Wheelchair access

How to Find Us

Located on the outskirts of Straffan village, Co. Kildare.

The Steam Museum is Ireland's only museum devoted to the Industrial Revolution, exhibiting working steam engines. The Victorian Gothic (c. 1865) building was re-structured from the Church of St. Jude at Inchicore built for employees of the Great Southern and Western Railway. It houses the Richard Guinness collection of inventors and prototype locomotive models including Trevithick's famous first four-wheeled self-propelled vehicle. The Power Hall displays stationary steam engines used or manufactured in Ireland.

Highlights of the Collection

Highlights include the original Third Model by Richard Trevithick, the first four-wheeled self-propelled vehicle in the world, which runs on high pressure steam and was popularly known as a "racing steam horse";

Inside the Steam Museum

the original prototype model of the Dublin to Kingston (Dun Laoghaire) railway locomotive and tender of 1834; and a full-sized single cylinder architectural beam engine from Smithwick's Brewery, Kilkenny.

Educational Programmes

The Museum is glad to encourage school groups. The children enjoy seeing the large size of the engines and learning how this early technology led to today's marvels, such as electrical generation, which has made computers possible.

Engine on display

The Museums of Munster

Bunratty Castle and Folk Park

Contact Information

Bunratty Folk Park
Co. Clare
Tel: 061 360788
Web: www.shannonheritage.com

Opening Hours

Open year round, 9.30 to 5.30
(9.00 to 6.00 in summer)
Admission fees: Adult, €11.00;
Children, €6.25; Family, €26.75

Facilities

Access and facilities for disabled
Picnic area
Restaurant, gift shop

How to Find Us

Located just off the main dual
carriageway between Shannon and
Limerick, the N18.

In order to build a jet runway at Shannon International Airport in the early 1960s, it was necessary to demolish a farmhouse which lay in its path. To save this small traditional Irish farmhouse from extinction, the timber and stones were salvaged and brought to Bunratty where the house was lovingly reconstructed brick by brick, thus heralding the birth of Bunratty Folk Park, located seven miles from Shannon Airport.

Bunratty Castle

specimen of the smaller farmhouse of the upland regions of West Limerick and North Kerry; and the wealthier farmer would have lived in a long thatched house (Golden Vale house) with a spacious kitchen and parlour.

A village street was added to the Folk Park, containing further examples of authentically recreated buildings from the nineteenth century including a post office, pawn brokers, schoolhouse, craft shops, doctor's surgery, draper's shop and — what no Irish village would be complete without — the village pub. MacNamara's, or "Mac's" as the pub has become affectionately known, is an exact copy of the original Kearney's Hotel in Ennis. Much of the furnishing and the fittings from the original hotel have been acquired and fitted. The pub is open all year round working normal pub hours and a full lunch time menu is served each day.

Gradually over the years many traditional farmhouses and cottages were built, all of them exact copies of buildings which existed in Ireland's Shannon region at the turn of the century. They have been furnished and decorated in the style of that time, with all the furniture in the houses being original.

Village Street

The houses tell a great deal about the Irish rural life style during the last century. The "Bothan Scoir" is an example of a poor labourer's dwelling. The Mountain Farmhouse is a

Two recent additions to the Folk Park are Ardcroney Church and Hazelbrook House.

Ardcroney Church, belonging to the Church of Ireland, was built c.1824 and used until 1986, when it was finally forced to close its doors due to a decline in the number of church goers. The church was falling into disrepair when it was decided to donate the church to be preserved at the Folk Park. Literally stone by stone, the church was moved from Ardcroney in Co. Tipperary to its new home in Bunratty.

Hazelbrook House was built in 1898 and was the home of the Hughes Brothers who started a dairy industry in the 1800s and later produced HB ice cream, which became, and still is, a household name in ice cream in Ireland. Inside the house visitors can learn about the evolution of ice cream making and trace the history of the industrious Hughes Brothers family.

Bunratty Folk Park is not an ordinary museum, with exhibits in a glass case — it actively keeps alive the memory of a culture and a way of life in danger of being forgotten with the passage of time.

The Folk Park is alive with activity, with Irish people clad in period costume practising traditional Irish skills in the settings in which they were nurtured. Butter making in a "dash" churn and soda-bread baking in a pot oven over an open turf fire can be observed, as can the blacksmith shoeing horses and donkeys. *A bean-a'-tighe* (woman of the house) welcomes guests and is al-ways eager to impart tales of Ireland "in the good old days".

Bunratty Castle at Night

Bunratty is alive at night as much as day where each night from April to October The Corn Barn is the venue for "the Traditional Irish Night", an evening of Irish music, dance, song, stories and laughter. The show interprets the story of Irish dance from early times through to contemporary Ireland. Entertainers dressed in traditional Irish costume demonstrate the art of Irish dancing and give visitors an opportunity to learn a few steps.

Mac's Pub, in the Village Street, also provides traditional Irish music on Wednesday nights from June to September. In the castle itself visitors can share, with up to 140 guests, a banquet with the Great Earl of Thomond, while being entertained by the world-renowned Shannon Heritage Singers.

Cape Clear Museum and Archive

Contact Information

Cape Clear Island
Co. Cork
Tel: 028 39119 or 021 4274110
Email: logainmneacha@yahoo.com
Web: www.placenames.ie/capeclear/
museum.html

Opening Hours

Open daily 12.00 to 5.00 from 1 June
to 31 August and from September to
May by arrangement.
Admission fee: €4.00

How to Find Us

Cape Clear Island is located 10 km
southwest of Baltimore. Ferry service
from Baltimore and Schull.

Cape Clear Museum is housed in a restored old schoolhouse and contains several hundred artefacts of island maritime and folklife interest. There are, to date, 196 framed exhibition panels in the collection which deal with fourteen different themes of island heritage. Each theme may have from six to fourteen exhibition panels, but only a few of these may be exhibited at any one time. The exhibition is changed each summer and anniversary and special exhibitions are also mounted.

Aspects covered in the exhibition panels include St. Ciarán/St. Piran: Pilgrim Islander, archaeology, placenames, shipwrecks, famine, education, genealogy, folk and farm, geology, lighthouses and signal towers, telegraphs, fishing, maritime history and folklore. The Fastnet Lighthouse and Fastnet Race of 1979 form a special exhibition.

Cape Clear Island Archive

Cape Clear Island Archive is a comprehensive collection of baptism, marriage and burial records, headstone inscriptions, school rolls, boat and land ownership lists, census returns, maps, folklore, placename and genealogical archive compiled over thirty years by Dr. Éamon Lankford. Also included is a compilation of some 2,200 photographs of island life which are individually catalogued in various themes. The Archive material will not be available to the public in both Cape Clear Museum and island library and Cork County Library until January 2007.

Cape Clear Island Museum

Celtic & Prehistoric Museum

Contact Information

Kilvicadownig, Ventry
Dingle, Co. Kerry
Tel: 066 9159191
Email: celticmuseum@hotmail.com
Web: www.celticmuseum.com

Opening Hours

Open from March to 15 November,
10.00 to 5.30.
Admission: Adults, €4.00; Children,
€2.50

Facilities

Café
Gift shop

How to Find Us

Located in Kilvicadownig, ten minutes west of Dingle.

In the Celtic and Prehistoric Museum, visitors can enter the Fossil Room and walk on floors of 300 million-year-old sea worms. They can see a large nest of 70–80 million-year-old dinosaur eggs, a group of 500 million-year-old squid and the largest complete woolly mammoth skull in the world – the tusks are each ten feet long!

Other highlights at the museum include fossil Ice Age beasts and authentic tools used by Homo Erectus, Neanderthal and Cro-Magnon man in the Cave Room. The walls are adorned with faithful reproductions of the oldest cave paintings in the world, accidentally discovered in France in 1994.

In the Neolithic Room visitors will see long flint axes used to clear the primeval forests of Europe 6,000 years ago. There is also 8,000 year old amber jewellery from Scandinavia, earth goddess figurines from Central Europe and stone battle axes and daggers introduced by invading horsemen from the east 4,500 years ago.

Bronze figurines, Celt-Iberian, c. third to fifth century AD

Upstairs there is a massive collection of Copper and Bronze Age ceremonial grave goods and another room filled with beautiful spiralling Celtic jewellery, weapons and even Viking ice skates made from bones!

70–80-million-year-old fossil dinosaur eggs

Double spiral arm guard, Central Europe, c. 1000 BC

119

"I think of art, at its most significant, as a DEW line, a Distant Early Warning system that can always be relied on to tell the old culture what is beginning to happen to it."

— Marshall McLuhan

Clare County Museum

Contact Information

Arthur's Row
Ennis, Co. Clare
Tel: 065 6823382
Email: claremuseum@clarecoco.ie
Web: www.clarelibrary.ie

Opening Hours

October to May
Tuesday to Saturday 9.30 to 1.00
and 2.00 to 5.00
June to September
Monday to Saturday 9.30 to 5.00
Sunday 2.00 to 5.00
Admission is free.

Facilities

Tourist information and gift shop
Disabled access

How to Find Us

Clare Museum is located in the centre of Ennis, at Arthur's Row, off O'Connell Square, adjacent to the Temple Gate Hotel. Visitors can also access the building via the Francis Street car park, adjacent to the Franciscan Friary.

The building within which the Clare Museum is housed was originally a Sisters of Mercy school and chapel. The congregation came to Ennis in 1854 at the invitation of Parish Priest Dean John Kenny. Row House, on the site of the present Temple Gate Hotel, was adapted for the use of the Sisters. A former occupant was Charles O'Connell, cousin of Daniel O'Connell, who often visited the house during his 1820s campaign for Catholic Emancipation. The sisters soon became involved in teaching. A new convent was built in 1861 to accommodate the growing number of sisters and Row House was incorporated into it.

The section that is now the Clare Museum was constructed as a prima-

Over 400 archaeological discoveries from Clare are on display

ry school in 1865 and the final portion of the convent complex, a chapel and classrooms, was erected in 1869. As well as schools, the order had an orphanage and several small industries. Sisters from Ennis convent established foundations overseas: in Connecticut (1872) and California (1859, 1963) in the United States; in New South Wales, Australia (1875) and Hokitika, New Zealand (1878). Branch houses and schools were also set up in Killaloe and Spanish Point, as well as in Colaiste Muire in the town of Ennis. The sisters acted as administrators and nurses in the workhouses in Ennis, Corofin and Roscrea. In 1995 the main convent building was demolished, with only the present section surviving. The sisters now live in smaller accommodation, but their work continues

The exhibition features original thematic paintings

and many of the schools which they founded still flourish.

The Riches of Clare

The Riches of Clare – its people, places, treasures – occupies two galleries of the Clare Museum. The displays have been designed to have a wide visitor appeal and comprise a large loan of artefacts of Clare provenance from the National Museum of Ireland, the de Valera Museum collection, and artefacts collected locally. The galleries incorporate the traditional method of displaying original artifacts with modern interpretive tools such as colourful display panels, audiovisual and computer interactive presentations, models, some replicas and specially commissioned art pieces. All showcases have been specifically designed with their contents in mind and environmentally conditioned to the requirements of the artefacts displayed in them. The concept of the exhibition is thematic, focusing on the lives and experiences of the people of Clare through the themes of Earth, Power, Faith, Water and Energy.

The Deputy Lieutenant of Clare's uniform

Cobh Museum

Contact Information

High Road
Cobh, Co. Cork
Tel: 021 4814240
Email: cobhmuseum@eircom.net
Web: www.cobhmuseum.com

Opening Hours

Open Easter to October, 11.00 to 1.00
and 2.00 to 5.00; Sunday, 3.00 to 6.00.
Admission: Adults €1.50; Seniors,
€0.75; Family, €3.75

Facilities

Gift shop

How to Find Us

Located in the former Presbyterian
church, known as Scots Church, in
Cobh.

The Cobh Museum is housed in the former Presbyterian Church known as "Scots Church". The building of this church was completed in 1854. Due to the declining number of parishioners in the area, it was closed for public worship in 1965 and donated to Cork County Council for cultural purposes. In 1970, under the guidance of the County Library Committee, it was made available to the Museum Committee formed by the Cobh ICA. It was opened as a museum in 1973. The main interior features of the church have survived including the pulpit, lectern, pews, harmonium and the original bible.

The displays in the museum reflect the maritime and cultural history of the town. The Great Island on which Cobh stands is the largest island in Cork Harbour. Cobh has had other names, Cove ("The Cove of Cork"), Queenstown (after the visit of Queen Victoria in 1849). It became Cobh after independence in 1922.

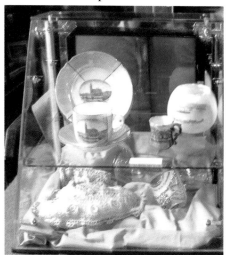

Display in Cobh Museum

Almost 40,000 men, women and young girls were transported from Cork Harbour. Millions left here dur-

Cobh Museum

ing and after the famine years. Cobh was the main transatlantic departure port in Ireland up to the late 1950s.

Highlights from the Collection

Highlights include the History of Spike Island, Secrets of Cork Harbour, Mementoes of a Victorian Lady, *Lusitania* memorabilia, paintings, watercolours, photographs, sporting heroes of Cobh, shipping pilots of Cork Harbour and models of local ships.

There is also a special genealogy area in the museum that is free for visitors to do their own research from the information available.

Cork Butter Museum

Contact Information

O'Connell Square
Shandon, Cork
Tel: 021 4300600
Email: info@corkbutter.museum
Web: www.corkbutter.museum

Opening Hours

March to October, 10.00 to 5.00 daily
(July to August, 10.00 to 6.00)
Admission fees: **Adults**, €3.50;
Students/Seniors, €2.50.

Facilities

Wheelchair access

How to Find Us

Located in the Tony O'Reilly Centre,
O'Connell Square, Cork.

The Cork Butter Museum is a unique institution. It tells the story of Ireland's most successful food industry, dairying, and Cork's greatest commercial enterprise, the Butter Exchange of the nineteenth century.

The visitor is introduced to the culture of cattle and dairying in Ireland from earliest times through the first upstairs gallery, which features a cask of early medieval bog butter, over a thousand years old.

The story of the development of the provisions trade in Cork, and particularly the growth of the Cork Butter Exchange, is dealt with in the second upstairs gallery. A combination of maps, models, display panels and original documents and artefacts describe the history of this commercial

Display at Cork Butter Museum

The traditional craft of home butter making is described in the downstairs gallery through a comprehensive collection of the objects used in the craft. The story is completed by a video documentary describing the revival of the dairy industry in the 1960s and 1970s through the formation of the Irish Dairy Board. Under its first general manager, Tony O'Reilly, and its first general secretary, Joe Cough, the Board went on to create and market "Kerrygold", one of Ireland's most successful international brands. Throughout the story, the visitor gets a picture of Ireland over the last fifty years, over which time the country has been transformed from a relatively poor country with low economic output to one of the most successful economies in Europe — a transformation in which the dairy industry played a significant part.

Display at Cork Butter Museum

phenomenon which, in its heyday, traded tens of millions of pounds of butter annually all over the world.

"People move forward into the future
out of the way they understand the past.
When we don't understand our past, we
are therefore crippled."

— Norman Mailer

Craggaunowen, The Living Past

Contact Information

Near Kilmurry
Co. Clare
Tel: 061 360788
www.shannonheritage.com

Opening Hours

Open daily April to mid-October
Admission: Adults, €7.85; Seniors
and Students, €5.85; Children, €4.75;
Family tickets available.

Facilities

Tea room
Gift shop
Limited wheelchair acceess

How to find us

Located off the N18. From Limerick
take the R462 from Cratloe and following Kilmurry turning left at the
R469. From Ennis take the R469.

Craggaunowen – the Living Past Experience is Ireland's original prehistoric park. Situated on 50 acres of wooded grounds, the Park interprets Ireland's prehistoric and early Christian eras. It recreates some of the homesteads, animals and artefacts which existed in Ireland over 1,000 years ago.

A major feature of the visit is the Crannóg (meaning "young tree") which is a reconstructed lake-dwelling of a type found in Ireland during the Iron Age and Early Christian periods. Some homesteads were inhabited during the Late Bronze Age and in some cases were still being occupied as late as the seventeenth century.

The site also includes a Ring Fort, of which there are about 40,000 examples throughout Ireland. It was the standard type of farmstead during the early Christian Period (fifth to twelfth centuries AD). Within the circular earthen bank or stone walls, the inhabitants carried out their everyday farmyard activities: they cooked over

Crannóg

open fires or in pits; corn was ground for making bread or porridge on hand-powered querns; pottery was made and wooden bowls, goblets and platters were turned on pole lathes.

Aerial view

The contemporaries of the people living in ring forts produced the magnificent artefacts of the Golden Age — the Ardagh Chalice, the Tara Brooch, the Book of Kells, the Derrynaflan Hoard and many other masterpieces.

Also featured is an "Iron Age Roadway" and an outdoor cooking site; and the renowned "Brendan Boat", a leather-hulled boat used to re-enact the Atlantic voyage of St Brendan and the early Christian monks reputed to have discovered America centuries before Columbus.

Highlights from the Collection

The Hunters' Cooking Site
The cooking site reconstructed here is a type that was common through-

out the country. Hunting parties used them over a long period of time, from the early Bronze Age to the Elizabethan period.

A rectangular hole was dug in low-lying land where it was sure to fill with water. This was clad on the four sides with wooden sections. Stones heated on the campfire were then used to boil the water in the wooden trough. A joint of venison was then wrapped in straw and put into the boiling water and cooked for a designated period.

The Brendan Boat

Another important attraction is the "Brendan Boat", the hide boat in which Tim Severin sailed from Ireland to the United States, re-enacting the Voyage of St Brendan the Navigator, reputed to have discovered America centuries before Columbus.

St Brendan the Navigator (who died c.583 AD) was, according to a ninth-century manuscript, *The Navigacio*, the first man to discover the "Promised Land" across the Atlantic. This place he called High Brasil and first came to him a dream.

The actual boat used in Severin's endeavour is on display in a specially constructed glass boathouse, reminiscent of a glacier – freezing the boat in timeless perpetuity.

The Souterrain

These underground passages were designed primarily as food storage areas. Ventilated, but draft-free, souterrains maintain a constant temperature of around four degrees no matter how hot it gets on the surface.

They could also be used as places of refuge during attacks on the ring fort. Many souterrains have secondary or tertiary chambers which are difficult to enter, thereby affording their occupants a measure of security.

Educational Programmes

A "Celtic Journey" is the core theme which takes visitors on an adventure through time. The story brings the

Brendan Boat

student into the magic and mystery of the prehistoric, Celtic, Viking, Anglo-Norman and native Irish societies starting 5,000 years ago and continuing to the present day.

"I said to myself, I'll paint what I see – what the flower is to me but I'll paint it big and they will be surprised into taking time to look at it. I will make even busy New Yorkers take time to see what I see of flowers."

— Georgia O'Keeffe

Crawford Municipal Art Gallery

Contact Information

Emmet Place
Cork
Tel: 021 4907855
Email: crawfordgallery@eircom.net
Web: www.crawfordartgallery.ie

Opening Hours

Monday to Saturday, 10.00 to 5.00
Admission is free

Facilities

Wheelchair access

How to Find Us

Located in Emmet Square next to the
Opera House.

The Crawford Municipal Art Gallery is one of Ireland's key art galleries providing an opportunity for an engaging and entertaining visit. The gallery dates from 1724 when it was first constructed as the Customs House for Cork. The building was converted into an art school early in the nineteenth century and a municipal art collection was established. A key part of this collection is a set of sculpture casts from the Vatican Museum, including works from Antonio Canova, which were brought to Cork in 1819. A magnificent extension designed by Arthur Hill housing studios and galleries was added in 1884, blending in well with the original building, and in June 2000 a new wing designed by Erick van Egeraat was added giving the his-

Uncovering art in Harry Clarke room

torical ensemble two new exhibition galleries. In total, over 3,000 square metres of new exhibition space has been added to the existing building, making the Crawford one of the most impressive galleries in Ireland. Over the past decade the Gallery has developed a comprehensive exhibitions programme giving exposure to both new and established talent. It hosts an average of twenty visiting

Gibson Bequest Gallery, part of the permanent collection

or temporary exhibitions a year seeking to develop an awareness, appreciation and understanding of the visual arts within the city and beyond. Its permanent collection focuses on Irish art from the eighteenth century to the present day and is constantly being added to through the purchases of new works of art.

Highlights from the Collection

At present the gallery is holding a major exhibition of the work of James Barry (1741–1806), the great historical painter. He was born and trained in Cork with many of his works now part of the permanent collection.

Joseph Stafford Gibson, a local property owner with a love of painting and travel, bequeathed almost

£15,000 to the Crawford Gallery in 1919, the proceeds to be used to acquire works by living Irish artists of the time. Due to this finance programme some fine examples of nineteenth and twentieth century were purchased including works by Jack B. Yeats, Sean Keating, Frank Bramley, W.J. Leech and Walter Osborne.

The Gibson Fund has brought over 200 works to the Gallery, not just paintings but also drawings, prints and sculptural pieces. These include a complete set of preparatory sketches for the Harry Clarke stained glass window *The Eve of St. Agnes*, the original of which is now on display in Dublin's Hugh Lane Municipal Gallery.

*Crawford Gallery –
Contemporary Façade*

Educational Programmes

Apart from guided visits specifically addressed to correspond with the secondary schools syllabus in Art,

Enlightening experiences in art during schools special programme

the gallery also works on other special educational programmes aimed at the primary schools in the city and surrounding counties. These provide children with guided tours of the permanent collection or temporary exhibitions and finishes with a workshop where two artists encourage and assist the children to express their reaction to the work through creating something (NB: prior booking only).

The month of May sees the Gallery and the Age & Opportunity organisation participate in a programme of education called Bealtaine, which is specifically designed for celebrating creativity in older age. This programme invites people to join in on tours, talks and workshops given by artists on special themes within the collection and enjoy a social cup of tea and scones afterwards.

"Of all national assets archives are the most precious; they are the gift of one generation to another and the extent of our care of them marks the extent of our civilization."

— *Sir Arthur George Doughty*

Foynes Flying Boat Museum

Contact Information

Foynes
Co Limerick
Tel: 069 65416
Email: famm@eircom.net
Web: www.flyingboatmuseum.com

Opening Hours

Open daily March 31 to October 31,
10.00 to 6.00 (last entry 5.00)
Admission fees: **Adult,** €7.50;
Children, €4.00; Family, €18.00

Facilities

Coffee shop
Souvenir shop
Wheelchair access

How to Find Us

Foynes is located 35 km west of
Limerick on the N69.

Foynes, Ireland, became the centre of the aviation world from 1939 to 1945. On 9 July 1939, Pan Am's luxury Flying Boat, the "Yankee Clipper" landed at Foynes. This was the first commercial passenger flight on a direct route from the USA to Europe. During the late 1930s and early 1940s, this quiet little town on the Shannon became the focal point for air traffic on the North Atlantic.

During this period, many famous politicians, international businessmen, film stars, active servicemen and wartime refugees passed through Foynes. In fact, the site was initially surveyed in 1933 by Colonel Charles Lindbergh and his wife Ann, who landed in Galway Bay flying his Lockheed Sirius. In December 1935, the *Irish Times* announced that Foynes would be the site for the European Terminal for transatlantic air services. Colonel Lindbergh returned again representing Pan Am in 1936 to inspect the facilities and also in 1937 to view the departure of "Clipper III".

The era of the flying boats was colourful but brief. In 1945, hundreds of people watched as Captain Blair piloted the last American Export flying boat out of Foynes to New York. Upon arrival, he turned

around and piloted the first landplane, a DC-4, back to open the new airport at Rineanna, later to

Foynes – The War Years

become Shannon International Airport. Shortly afterward, Pan Am, after 2,097 Atlantic crossings through Foynes, made their last flight to Lisbon from Foynes. Only a day before, their first landplane had also landed at Rineanna.

The photograph on the previous page shows the Pan Am's Boeing 314 "Atlantic Clipper" NC 18604 on take-off. The Clipper first flew through Foynes on 28 August 1939. Saturday, 18 August 1945, was a record day for Pan American World Airways operations in Foynes. Two clippers, the "Atlantic" and the "Dixie" arrived from New York in the morning and returned that night. A total of 101 transatlantic passengers were handled at the airport — a record for a day's operation by one airline. Among the arriving passengers were Mr Michael Prendergast of Claremorris, County Mayo and Ms Margaret Sheehan, a nurse from Carparoe, Nenagh. Also travelling were nationals from Great Britain, Argentina, Sweden, Switzerland, France, Czechoslovakia, Netherlands and the US. Among the departing passengers were Ray Milland of Hollywood fame; Harry Dietz of Du Pont (the entomologist who was largely responsible for the development of the revolutionary insecticide DDT); and Mrs Dorothy Rosenmann, wife of the legal advisor to President Truman.

About the Museum

The Foynes Flying Boat Museum has a comprehensive range of exhibits and graphic illustrations. Visitors can travel back in time in the authentic 1940s cinema, while watching the award-winning film "Atlantic Conquest". The museum showcases the original Terminal Building, Radio and Weather Room, complete with transmitters, receivers and Morse code equipment. The exhibits feature an introduction to the first transatlantic passenger service and Foynes during the war years.

Located at the west end of Foynes, the museum is housed in the original old terminal building, which was formerly the Monteagle Arms Hotel. The property was built in the 1860s and was the first public bar and hotel in Foynes before becoming the headquarters for aviation for Ireland. Prior to 1980 it was an Irish college, at which time it was renamed "Áras Íde".

Inside the Foynes Flying Boat Museum

Highlights of the Collection

The highlights from the Foynes Flying Boat Museum inlcude: the 17 minute film, *Atlantic Conquest*, which contains all original footage; memorabilia and artefacts from the pioneering age of air passenger travel; a flight simulator of the Boeing 314; and original radio and weather equipment still in working condition.

Future Developments

The Museum is presently completing a €1.5 million development to include building a full-scale model of the Boeing 314, which will be the only one in the world.

"Museums . . . are also sources of pleasure and inspiration. Doubtless it will seem strange to many that the hand unaided by sight can feel action, sentiment, beauty in the cold marble; and yet it is true that I derive genuine pleasure from touching great works of art. As my fingertips trace line and curve, they discover the thought and emotion which the artist has portrayed."

— Helen Keller

The Hunt Museum

Contact Information

The Custom House
Rutland Street
Limerick
Tel: 061 312833
Email: info@huntmuseum.com
Web: www.huntmuseum.com

Opening Hours

Monday to Saturday, 10.00 to 5.00
Sunday, 2.00 to 5.00
Admission fees: **Adult,** €7.20;
Children, €3.50; Family, €16.50

Facilities

Restaurant
Gift shop
Wheelchair access

How to Find Us

Located in Limerick City, three minutes' walk from the Tourist Office.

The Hunt Collection is housed in Limerick city's finest eighteenth century building, the Custom House, an elegant Palladian-style building designed by the Franco-Italian architect Davis Ducart. This Collection contains a dazzling assemblage of objects and makes Limerick into one of the "must be visited" cultural centres of both Ireland and Europe. John and Gertrude Hunt selected each piece in the Collection according to the quality of its design, craftsmanship and artistic merit. It is not just the big names such as Picasso, Renoir, Gauguin and da Vinci which afford the Hunt Collection its legendary status, but also the superb quality of the work on display by anonymous craftsmen. Each piece encourages a sense of curiosity and wonder.

The cultures of ancient Egypt, Greece and Rome are well represented as are Irish archaeological treasures such as the Antrim Cross of c.800. This is one of the rare bronze crosses to survive virtually intact from one of the greatest periods of Irish craftsmanship. The Collection also features many items of medieval religious art from all over Europe. Walking through the galleries the list of interesting objects is endless. Visitors can admire jewellery, porcelain, sculpture, reliquaries, paintings, table silver or glass.

Illustrating the progression of craftsmanship and the decorative

arts through the ages, people's craftsmanship is what the Hunt Museum celebrates. The Hunt family gener-

The Hunt Museum

ously donated the collection to the people of Ireland so that the interest and pleasure they derived from it might be shared by as many people as possible. John Hunt believed a nation's past to be part of its soul and that to enrich a people they must be given a respect and true understanding of the past.

Highlights from the Collection

The Hunt Museum houses a diverse collection of antiquities and fine and decorative art. It reflects the tastes and interests of the two people who formed it, John and Gertrude Hunt. There are artefacts from Greece, Rome, Egypt and the Olmec civilisation. There is also an important collection of Irish archaeological material ranging from Neolithic flints and Bronze Age material, including a Bronze Age shield and cauldron, to later Christian objects such as the

Apollo, German, seventeenth century, polychromed limewood

unique ninth century Antrim Cross. One of the strengths of the collection is its medieval material, which include statues in stone and wood, painted panels, jewellery, enamels, ivories, ceramics, crystal and crucifixes. Decorative arts from the eighteenth and nineteenth century are also represented with fine examples of silver, glass and ceramics. Artists in the collection include Pablo Picasso, Pierre Auguste Renoir, Roderic O'Connor, Jack B. Yeats, Robert Fagan and Henry Moore.

Primary Schools Programme

The Primary Schools Programme consists of specially devised tours, workshops and activities for all ages at primary level:

- Hunt Museum Treasure Trail
- Seasonal Treasure Trails
- Painting with words
- Portrait
- Drawing in the Galleries
- Time Travel workshop
- Costume workshop
- Stone Age workshop
- Life in the Medieval World
- Holy Communion workshop
- Portrait workshop.

The Education Department at the Museum also offers a comprehensive Secondary Schools' Programme, Docent Programme and Liberal Arts course.

Triptych: Painted Epitaph, German or Flemish, assembled after 1611

Irish Palatine Museum

Contact Information

Old Railway Buildings
Rathkeale, Co. Limerick
Tel: 069 63511
Email: ipass@eircom.net
Web: www.irishpalatines.org

Opening Hours

Open 16 May to 16 September,
Tuesday to Saturday and Bank
Holiday Mondays, 2.00 to 5.00;
other times by prior appointment.
Admission: Adults, €5.00; Students,
€3.00; Family, €12.00.

Facilities

Café
Gift shop
Wheelchair access

How to Find Us

Located alongside the N21 at
Rathkeale, 29 km from Limerick City.

In 1709 several hundred families of German origin settled in Ireland. Known as the Palatines, they established roots mainly in Counties Limerick, Kerry, Tipperary and Wexford. From there they emigrated to many parts of the English-speaking world including Australia, Canada, England, New Zealand and the United States.

The centre houses an exhibition which seeks to represent in detail the Irish Palatine experience ranging from their German places of origin to their colonisation and settlement in Ireland, and their subsequent scattering all over the English-speaking world.

Due emphasis is placed on the Palatines' innovative contributions to Irish farming life and on their formative role in the development of world Methodism.

The Centre features an extensive display of artefacts, photographs, graphics etc. associated with the Palatine story. It is set in landscaped surroundings and includes an ar-

Palatine costumes

chive, a tea room, gift selection and bus/car park.

Highlights from the Collection

Highlights include examples of clothes worn by the Irish Palatines, items from their homes, examples of Palatine needle work, a large collection of personal documents belonging to their principal landlord, letters belonging to members of Irish Palatines who emigrated to Australia and North America in the 1800s, and legal and other documents pertaining to agreements between families dating from 1760 onwards.

Horn used to call Palatine people together

New Developments/Future Plans

Future plans include an extension of the exhibition to further illustrate the Irish Palatine story and to make it more friendly for speakers of German and other languages; extension of the library to better facilitate those doing genealogical and other research on the Irish Palatines; restoration of the goods railway building to facilitate improvements; and production of an audio-visual presentation.

Educational/Special Programmes

To date the museum has successfully accommodated groups of all school levels and of all denominations.

The museum offers a relaxed yet educational presentation, which not alone introduces visitors to this story in Irish history, but also relates to such ever-present topics as prejudice, poverty, religious intolerance and the ability of the human to overcome adversity.

The story connects with prominent characters in history such as Louie XIV, Daniel Defoe and Jonathan Swift.

Additional Comments

The Irish Palatine Association was formed to:

• Encourage and develop a sense of identity among Palatine families and their descendants.

• Collect and preserve original documents, photographs and memorabilia relating to Palatine families and to act as trustees of such material for posterity.

• Make contact and develop links with descendants of Palatines everywhere.

• Signpost and identify sites associated with the Irish Palatine Story.

Kerry County Museum

Contact Information

Ashe Memorial Hall
Denny Street
Tralee, Co. Kerry
Tel: 066 7127777
Email: info@kerrymuseum.ie
Web: www.kerrymuseum.ie

Opening Hours

January to March, Tuesday to Friday,
10.00 to 4.30;
April to May, Tuesday to Saturday,
9.30 to 5.30;
June to August, daily, 9.30 to 5.30;
September to December, Tuesday to
Saturday, 9.30 to 5.00

Admission fees: **Adult,** €8.00;
Student/Senior, €6.50; Children, €5.00

Facilities

Restaurant
Book shop
Wheelchair access

How to Find Us

Located in the town centre of Tralee.

Kerry County Museum brings to life the story of Kerry from the earliest times to the present day. Priceless treasures are on display in the museum, illustrating the rich heritage of the county. Visitors can travel back 600 years in the Geraldine Experience to see, hear and smell medieval Tralee. Kerry in Colour takes them on a panoramic visual tour, showing the people and places of the Kingdom of Kerry.

Kerry County Museum is located in the Ashe Memorial Hall, a fine example of public architecture in the centre of Tralee. The building is named after Thomas Ashe, a Kerryman who was a member of the Irish Volunteers and who died on hunger strike while imprisoned in Mountjoy

Arrowhead

in 1917. The Ashe Hall was designed by Thomas J. Cullen and built with local sandstone. It was completed in

1928 and, for more than half a century, it was the administrative head-

Crozier

quarters of Kerry County Council and Tralee Urban District Council. In the 1980s both local authorities moved to new offices and the building was transformed into Kerry County Museum, opening its doors to the public in 1992.

The museum gallery follows a chronological route. Beginning with the first settlers in the Late Mesolithic site at Ferriter's Cove on the Dingle Peninsula, visitors encounter the archaeology and history of Kerry. Each artefact has its own story to tell, whether it is a beautiful sunflower pin worn by the fashion-conscious in the Bronze Age, or duelling pistols used by the Liberator, Daniel O'Connell, in the early nineteenth century.

The aim of the museum is to collect, record, preserve and display the material heritage of Co. Kerry. Under the National Monuments Act (1994) and the National Cultural Institutions Act (1997), Kerry County Museum is a designated repository for archaeological artefacts in Co. Kerry. The museum continues to develop, adding to its collection by donation, acquisition and loan.

The Medieval Experience

The Medieval Experience takes visitors back in time to Geraldine Tralee in 1450. The term "Geraldine" comes from the name Fitzgerald, and the Fitzgeralds were one of the original Norman families that invaded Ireland in the late twelfth century.

The Fitzgeralds took lands in Limerick and north Kerry, founding the town of Tralee in 1216. Like all the Norman families, the Fitzgeralds were enthusiastic patrons of the church and the great European monastic orders were invited to Ireland to open houses in those areas under Norman control.

The Dominicans were invited to Tralee and their priory was opened in the town in 1243. By 1450 the Fitzgeralds were Earls of Desmond, controlling a vast amount of territory throughout Munster.

Although nothing remains of the original priory, great castle or town walls, visitors have the chance to experience medieval life in Geraldine Tralee. They will experience all the sights, sounds and smells of a medieval town on their journey through the streets, port, abbey and castle of Tralee in 1450.

Portrait of Daniel O'Connell

Why Museums?

"Museums sharpen our vision of the world. They encourage wonder and understanding, knowledge and play. They enable us to recover many different pasts, review the plurality of the present and imagine myriad futures. They create connections and reveal to us how intertwined we are with each other and the world around us."

— Fiona Kearney, Director, Lewis Glucksman Gallery

Lewis Glucksman Gallery

Contact Information

University College Cork
Cork
Tel: 021 4901844
Email: info@glucksman.org
Web: www.glucksman.org

Opening Hours

Tuesday to Saturday, 10.00 to 5.00
Late night Thursday until 8.00
Sunday 12.00 to 5.00
Closed Mondays
Admission is free

Facilities

Wheelchair access

How to Find Us

Located on the campus of University College Cork, just behind the Ceremonial Gates entrance to UCC on the Western Road, a short walk from the city centre.

The Lewis Glucksman Gallery is a cultural and educational institution that promotes the research, creation and exploration of the visual arts. The gallery is named in honour of American financier and philanthropist Lewis Glucksman and was inaugurated on 15 October 2004 by President Mary McAleese. Located at University College Cork's main entrance on Western Road, the Glucksman is a landmark building that includes temporary exhibition display spaces, lecture facilities, a riverside restaurant and gallery shop.

On 2 June 2005, the Glucksman was named Best Public Building in Ireland by the RIAI. The building is a RIBA award winner and was one of six buildings shortlisted for the UK's most prestigious architecture award, The Stirling Prize.

The Glucksman's artistic mission is to explore all aspects of visual culture and present a range of innovative and intellectually stimulating displays. The exhibitions programme at the Glucksman fosters scholarship in a new environment placing particular emphasis on the unique role of visual media in communicating knowledge. Central to this is the creation of discursive relationships between academic disciplines and art practice. This is reflected in a wide range of exhibitions that span various media and historical periods.

Previous exhibitions include "Modern American Painting from the NYU Art Collection"; "Dürer's Indecision: The North-South Dichot-

Lewis Glucksman Gallery

omy in the Prints of Albrecht Dürer"; "40 Shades of Green: A Convergence of Irish Art and Craft"; "Through the Looking Glass: Childhood in Contemporary Photography"; "Blake & Sons: Alternative Lifestyles and Mysticism in Contemporary Art".

Highlights from the Collection

The art collection of University College Cork is administered by the Lewis Glucksman Gallery. The University Art Collection concentrates on contemporary Irish art and now features many of Ireland's most distinguished practitioners. In addition to collecting significant works, UCC aims to support emerging artists in the region through the acquisition of new works for the collection and it sponsors an annual purchase prize at the Crawford College of Art degree show.

The University's art collection is displayed across campus in public buildings, teaching areas and in the college grounds. Occasionally, the Glucksman works with the collection for temporary exhibitions and both a catalogue of the collection and an education pack on the collection are available to purchase in the Glucksman shop.

Educational Programmes

The Lewis Glucksman Gallery places education at the heart of its activities with a wide range of art workshops, film screenings, seminars, lecture series and gallery tours on offer throughout the year. The Glucksman's education programme enables visitors to explore the artistic programme in greater depth.

The Glucksman also presents a special schools programme that supports and enhances the national curriculum. One of the key objectives of the education programme is to situate children in a university setting at an early age, encouraging them to view third-level education as an accessible and desirable prospect.

Gallery 1

"One of the wonderful things about a museum is how you're jolted into confronting art from strange and wonderful civilizations and you look and learn and expand your horizons."

— Sister Wendy Beckett

Limerick City Gallery of Art

Contact Information

Carnegie Building
Pery Square
Limerick
Tel: 061 310633
Email: artgallery@limerickcity.ie
Web: www.limerickcity.ie/LCGA

Opening Hours

Open Monday to Friday, 10.00 to 6.00
Thursday, 10.00 to 7.00; Saturday,
10.00 to 5.00; Sunday, 2.00 to 5.00.
Admission is free

How to Find Us

Located in the Georgian area at the
People's Park, at the corner of Mallow
Street and Pery Square close to the
Railway Station.

John Lavery, "Stars in Sunlight"

Limerick City Gallery of Art was founded in 1948 as a purpose-built addition to the Carnegie Free Library and Museum, a 1906 Neo-Hiberno-Romanesque styled building adjacent to the Peoples Park and the Georgian-styled Pery Square, Limerick. The whole building became the Limerick City Gallery of Art in 1985, and recently a new South Wing Gallery was added.

LCGA has a fine permanent collection of works by early eighteenth, nineteenth and twentieth century Irish artists, which encourages one to trace the development of modern Irish art in painting, sculpture and drawing. The collection, begun in 1948, continues to grow each year. The Gallery also hosts exciting contemporary exhibitions by Irish and international artists including the widely known ev+a exhibition. Highlights include a fine collection of Irish art, such as William Orpen's *Man of the West*, a portrait of Sean Keating, Sean Keating's *Simple Folk*,

Grace Henry, Top of the Hill

works by Grace Henry such as *Top of the Hill* and Paul Henry's *Scene in Connemara*, Jack B. Yeats's *Chairoplanes*, George Barrett's *Powerscourt House*, Nathanial Hone's *Fishing Smacks* and Sir John Lavery's *Stars in Sunlight*. There are over 900 artworks in all.

Contemporary works include the National Collection of Contemporary Drawing, and paintings by John Shinnors, Donald Teskey, Gavin Hogg, Camile Souter, sculpture by Dorothy Cross and Tom Fitzgerald and many more.

Paul Henry, Scene in Connemara

Limerick City Museum

Contact Information

Castle Lane, Nicholas Street
Limerick
Tel: 061 417826
Email: lwalsh@limerickcity.ie
Web: www.limerickcity.ie

Opening Hours

Open all year, Tuesday to Saturday,
10.00 to 1.00; and 2.15 to 5.00
Admission is free

Facilities

Wheelchair access

How to Find Us

Located next to King John's Castle in
the city centre.

Limerick City Museum first opened to the public in 1916 as part of the City Library, with the city librarian of the day as curator. Pressure for library space led to its closure in 1974, and in 1979 it reopened with its own staff and premises in newly restored Queen Anne style houses at John's Square. In 1999 it moved to its present premises, a granary-style building beside King John's Castle.

Winner of the first Gulbenkian Irish Museum of the Year Award in 1992, it is a general regional museum housing more than 40,000 objects illustrating all aspects of the past of Limerick City and surrounding areas from earliest times to the present day. Its entire catalogue is searchable on the Limerick City Council website. It is one of twelve local authority museums around the country designated under the National Monuments Acts to collect archaeological material from its own area.

Ceremonial Apron of Limerick Slater's Guild, c. 1858

Highlights from the Collection

Highlights include Limerick silver of the eighteenth and nineteenth centuries, Limerick lace of the nineteenth century, the history of Limerick City Council, local printing of the eighteenth and nineteenth centuries, local manufacturers, local aspects of national independence movements from the eighteenth century, old postcards, prints, topographical paintings and photographs. One floor of the display is devoted to finds from the Abbey River — an arm of the Shannon which divides the medieval city in two — which was drained in the late 1990s and its bed excavated as a dry land archaeological site.

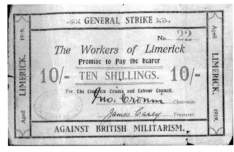

Currency note issued by Limerick Trades Council during the strike against British militarism, April 1919

Sirius Arts Centre

Contact Information

The Old Yacht Club Building
Cobh, Co. Cork
Tel: 021 4813790
Email: cobharts@iol.ie
Web: www.iol.ie/~cobharts

Opening Hours

Wednesday to Friday, 11.00 to 5.00;
Saturday and Sunday, 2.00 to 5.00
Admission is free

Facilities

Wheelchair access

How to Find Us

Located in the town of Cobh three minutes from the train station. The gallery is located on the harbour on the West side of the promenade in the middle of town.

Sirius Arts Centre is a multidisciplinary non-profit centre for the arts in the East Cork area. Founded in 1988, it is dedicated to facilitating artistic expression in Ireland. The centre's yearly programming is focused on raising artistic awareness and providing opportunities for participation in and enjoyment of the arts. This is achieved through a mix of activities including visual arts, a prestigious artists-in-residence programme, music, community arts and literature programmes. The Sirius Arts Centre building, which is currently being restored, provides the organisation with a unique environ-

The aims and objectives of the organisation are to develop, encourage and raise the level of arts practice in

Cobh Women's Group

Ireland, building international contacts and networking opportunities for artists and the community through Sirius Arts Centre's Artist in Residency and exhibition programme. It plans to do this by raising awareness, encouraging participation and providing opportunities for critical engagement in the arts across a broad social framework through monthly programming in varied arts disciplines and by linking with other arts-based organisations, local, national and international authorities and community groups. Also planned is continued restoration and revitalisation of Sirius Arts Centre's heritage building in order to provide a unique environment for all of the above.

View from window of West Gallery

ment, and the cultural programme gives continuing life to a heritage building of architectural and historical importance.

Highlights from the Collection

Sirius Arts Centre does not house a permanent collection as part of its exhibition programme but instead runs a yearly programme of exhibitions and other events featuring work by emerging professional artists from Ireland and abroad. In the past Sirius has hosted exhibitions by artists such as Simon Norfolk, Hendrike Kuhn and Beat Klein, Kim Jones, Martin Parr, Robert and Shana ParkeHarrison, Ellen Harvey, Hisao Suzuki, Mark Clare and Katie Holton, to name a few.

New Developments

In 2006 Sirius will invite a number of international artists to develop new work in Ireland through its Artist in Residency programme, and will also host exhibitions by a number of local, national and international emerging artists. Residencies will include Meridel Rubenstein, Reiner Reidler, Viv Corringham, Daniel Heer and others. Exhibitions will include a group show by Richochet, Brian Flynn, Reiner Reidler and others. In addition, the Centre will run a regular series of music concerts and community arts events. Sirius will also organise the Third Cobh Maritime song festival in June 2006, a weekend event that celebrates the colourful history of Cobh and Cork Harbour in music and storytelling featuring maritime musicians and performers from Ireland and abroad.

Educational Programmes

In 2006 Sirius Arts Centre will work on developing a community arts/ education programme with local schools, community groups and its international Artist in Residence programme looking at themes of regeneration/revitalisation at a local level. Artists participating in this programme will include David Jacques, Viv Corringham and Danny McCarthy.

Central gallery during an exhibition

Waterford County Museum

Contact Information

Old Town Hall, St Augustine Street
Dungarvan, Co Waterford
Tel 058-45960
Email: history@waterfordcounty
museum.org
Web: www.waterfordcounty
museum.org

Opening Hours

Monday to Friday, 10.00 to 5.00
Open Saturdays, June to September,
1.00 to 5.00
Admission is free.

Facilities

Gift shop
Wheelchair access

How to Find Us

Located opposite the Augustinian
Church in Dungarvan.

*Oil painting of "The Annette",
wrecked 1905*

Waterford County Museum is run by Waterford County Museum Society which is a non-profit voluntary organisation. The aims of the Society are to preserve the history of County Waterford; acquire, record and preserve individual items and collections of local interest; encourage public interest in local history; and publish various books and pamphlets on subjects of historical and local interest.

The museum has two websites, waterfordcountymuseum.org, which contains 3,500+ pages of Waterford history, and waterfordcountyimages.org, which contains 2,000+ images of Co. Waterford and was recently awarded Best Small Museum Website 2006 at the Museums and the Web International Conference.

Postcard showing the Dungarvan Coat of Arms

Waterford Artillery Dress Sword, early nineteenth century

Highlights from the Collection

The collection has a strong maritime theme reflecting the town's past as a centre for fishing, boat building and trade. On display are models, paintings, documents, photographs and other maritime memorabilia. Other areas covered include sport. The first cycling club in Ireland was founded in Dungarvan in 1867 and the cup awarded that year for the first cycle race is on display. Special temporary displays are mounted each year. These have included photography, business and industry, 1798 Rebellion, World War I, maps, etc.

New Developments

The Museum is to undergo a major reconstruction which will increase the display area significantly, enabling it to display many objects previously held in storage.

Educational Programmes

The Museum Society plans to introduce a programme for schools and as part of our outreach programme we currently have a travelling photographic exhibition touring the towns and villages of Co. Waterford.

Waterford Museum of Treasures

Contact Information

The Granary, Merchants Quay
Waterford
Tel: 051 304500
Email: granarymail@waterfordcity.ie
Web: www.waterfordtreasures.com

Opening Hours

April to September, Monday to
 Saturday, 9.30 to 6.00, Sunday, 11.00
to 6.00; October to March, Monday to
Saturday, 10.00 to 5.00, Sunday,
11.00 to 5.00.
Admission fees: **Adult,** €7.00;
Senior/Student, €5.00;
Family, €15.00–€21.00

Facilities

Restaurant
Gift shop
Wheelchair access

How to Find Us

Located on Waterford's historic
quays, next to bus station and tourist
office.

The Waterford Museum of Treasures celebrates the ethnic, cultural and religious diversity of all who contributed to the making of Waterford, Ireland's oldest city, from the Viking period to the end of the nineteenth century. The award-winning museum was opened in 1999 and offers a high-tech and modern experience through seven audiovisual presentations, three interactive pods and a soundguide in six different languages.

IV to the Mayor of Waterford in 1462, the Waterford Magi Cope made in Florence in 1480, oldest cannon gun

Kite Brooch Gallery

Highlights from the Collection

Highlights at the museum include a Viking age kite brooch, a Viking age gaming board and pieces, thirteenth-century yew bowstave, gold ring brooch, Great Charter Roll of 1372, ceremonial sword given by Edward

in Ireland, Cap of Maintenance and accompanying sword given by King Henry VIII to the Mayor of Waterford, Ireland's finest complete set of royal charters (1215–1815), French and Spanish seventeeth- and eighteenth-century silver plates, heirlooms of the Bonaparte Wyse family, Ireland's finest collection of eighteenth- and nineteenth-century Waterford glass, uniform and regalia of Thomas Francis Meagher and much more.

New Developments

Two major temporary exhibitions are to be mounted in 2006: one will chronicle the show-band era in the city when

Medieval Gallery

Waterford bands such as the Royal Showband dominated the scene. The second exhibition will focus on recent archaeological discoveries in the southeast with particular emphasis on the internationally important Viking site of Woodstown.

Educational/Special Programmes

There are active education, conservation and Friends of Waterford Museum of Treasures programmes. Guided tours by highly trained staff, geared to age and ability of the group, include worksheets, handling reproduction objects, striking a facsimile reproduction medi-

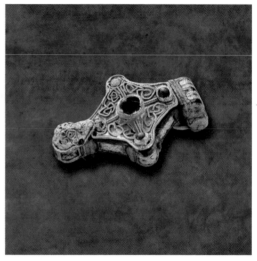

The Waterford Kite Brooch, c.1100 AD

eval Waterford coin and re-enactors demonstrating their skills. There is ongoing conservation of important objects from the collection.

Children having fun with reproduction weapons

The Museums of Ulster

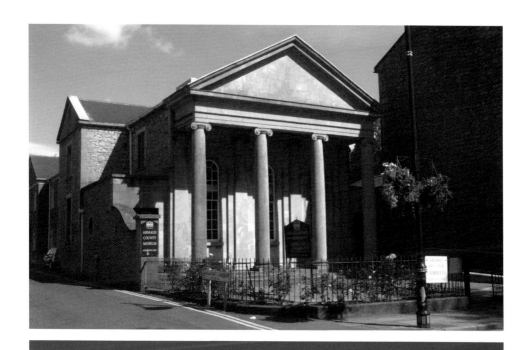

Armagh County Museum

Contact Information

The Mall East
Armagh BT61 9BE
Tel: 028 37523070
Email: acm.info@magni.org.uk
Web: ww.armaghcountymuseum.org.uk

Opening Hours

Monday to Friday, 10.00 to 5.00;
Saturday, 10.00 to 1.00
and 2.00 to 5.00.
Admission is free.

Facilities

Gift shop
Wheelchair acceess

How to find us

From Belfast follow the signs
through Portadown for Armagh.
On entering the city the museum is
located about half way along the
Mall, between the old gaol and the
courthouse.

Strolling along the tree-lined Mall, near the centre of St Patrick's cathedral city, a visit to Armagh County Museum is an ideal way to experience a flavour of the orchard county. Originally a school house, built in 1834 to a classical design, its impressive columns dominate the entrance, making it one of the most distinctive buildings in the area.

This is the oldest county museum in Ireland where on the ground floor visitors will find a shop and a sample of objects and paintings from the collections. The main displays and temporary exhibitions are on the upper floor accessible by stairs or lift.

Victorian dress

Highlights from the Collections

The museum's extensive collections and displays reflect the lives of people who have lived and worked in Armagh or have been associated with the county. Visitors will discover a rich and varied legacy revealed

Early fireman's helmet

in objects ranging from prehistoric artefacts to household items from a bygone age. There are military uniforms, wedding dresses, ceramics, natural history specimens and railway memorabilia. An impressive art collection includes works by many well-known Irish artists.

New Developments

Over the years, temporary exhibitions have introduced the music of the pipes, offered a nostalgic railway journey through the county and provided an accessible venue for local artists to display their work. This work continues with a landmark exhibition in 2006 celebrating Armagh and marking 150 years of a Museum on the Mall.

Education

A particular focus of the museum's education programme is geared towards helping primary schools. In addition to the range of temporary exhibitions the museum offers a series of workshops based around the primary school curriculum. These take place in the museum and use objects and resources from the collections.

Workshops offered include:

- Toys
- Life in Early Times
- Victorian School Days
- Life in the Recent Past
- Vikings

The museum also has an extensive reference library, rich in local archive material, along with photographic and map collections. With a range of changing exhibitions throughout the year, it is an ideal place to see and explore the fair county of Armagh.

Additional Comments

Visitors can take a quick tour of the museum, read articles from the newsroom and check details of the

Pocket Watch

latest events by visiting their website, www.armaghcountymuseum.org.uk. Armagh County Museum is part of the National Museums Northern Ireland.

Detail of straw work — a harvest knot

171

Ballycastle Museum

Contact Information

59 Castle Street,
Ballycastle, Co. Antrim
Tel: 028 20762942
Email: info@moyle-council.org
Web: www.moyle-council.org

Opening Hours

July and August,
Monday to Saturday 12.00 to 6.00
Admission is free.

How to find us

Located in the town centre of
Ballycastle.

Pleaskin Head *by A. Nicholl RHA (1804–1886)*

Ballycastle Museum was opened by Moyle District Council in 1976. In 1983 the Clarke collection, now known as the Irish Home Industries collection, was donated. Today the museum includes a display of objects from that collection which dates back to 1904 and is located within an eighteenth-century listed building, formerly the Market Building and Courthouse. There is also material on display that highlights the industrial development of Ballycastle by Hugh Boyd during eighteenth century, the "Oul' Lammas Fair", Marconi's work and more recently, the twentieth century social and commercial activity in the town including the Taisie Banner from the first Glens Feis in 1904. Moyle District Council is a partner in the Causeway Museum Service with Coleraine, Limavady and Ballymoney Borough Councils.

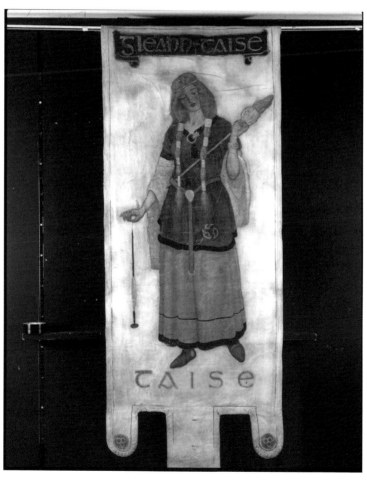

The Taisie Banner 1904 carried in the First Glens Feis

"Art does not solve problems but makes us aware of their existence. It opens our eyes to see and our brain to imagine."

— Magdalena Abakanowicz

Belfast Exposed Photography

Contact Information

The Exchange Place
23 Donegall Street
Belfast BT1 2FF
Tel: 028 9023 0965
Email: info@belfastexposed.org
Web: www.belfastexposed.org

Opening Hours

Tuesday to Saturday, 11.00 to 5.00 ;
Admission is free.

Facilities

Access and facilities for disabled visitors

How to find us

Based in Belfast city centre's historic Cathedral Quarter, 50 yards from St Anne's Cathedral.

Belfast Exposed Photography was established in 1983, traditionally focusing on the development and exhibition of community photography, placing the emphasis on dark-room workshops and on ways in which photographic seeing can contribute to self-esteem and foster social and political perspectives. The organisation primarily existed as a means to empower local communities by example and training to reflect on their past, record their present and to highlight and share concerns and achievements through the medium of photography.

Projects and Activities

Belfast Exposed is a photographic resource, archive and gallery; it remains

Claudio Hils from the series
"Archive, Belfast" 2004

Northern Ireland's only dedicated photography gallery. The Exchange Place (23 Donegall Street) now houses

Installation Topography of Titanic by Kai-Olaf Hesse

a 7x20 metre gallery for the exhibition of contemporary photography, a spacious black-and-white photographic darkroom and an eight-person Apple Mac digital suite.

Through its annual programme of exhibitions and the commissioning of new work, Belfast Exposed promotes excellence, access and participation in the arts and aims to raise the profile of photography as an art form. Belfast Exposed's policy of project origination places its main emphasis on the commissioning of new work, production of publications and generation of discussion through seminars and talks around projects.

Through a policy of retaining the negatives from community projects,

Belfast Exposed has compiled an archive of 500,000 images over the past two decades, providing a social document which records a turbulent historical period through the eyes and lenses of its principal actors, the communities themselves. Belfast Exposed has made an initial edit of 5,000 negatives, which are being critically examined and contextualised and are being made available online.

John Duncan from the series "Trees from Germany" 2003

New Developments

Belfast Exposed Photography is pioneering the development of a radically new audio interpretive system for galleries and museums in partnership with the Sonic Arts Research Centre at Queens University, Belfast and supported by Adapt NI. Specifically designed for use by people with visual impairments but available to all gallery users, the system proposes to treat the gallery as a soundscape environment in which images exist in relationship to one another. Breaking with traditional more linear modes of audio description, this system will give visitors choices in how they view and interact with the exhibition – they can view the work entirely unmediated if they wish, or select different levels of interpretation from straightforward descriptions to complex sound environments.

Michelle Sank from the series "Teenagers Belfast", 2005

Educational Programmes

Belfast Exposed Photography operates a unique training package offering hands-on experience in 35mm photography to both individuals and community groups. It enables the exploration of ideas, themes and issues through a creative and challenging process. It provides participants with practical photographic skills including processing and printing, location work, digital photography (scanning and Adobe Photoshop), editing and exhibition planning and promotion. Belfast Exposed offers structured training from short introductory courses to a comprehensive 14 session training programme, and has worked successfully with groups representing a broad range of interests from right across Northern Ireland.

Daniel Jewesbury and Ursula Burke from the series "Archive: Lisburn Road", 2004

Carrickfergus Museum

Contact Information

11 Antrim Street, Carrickfergus,
Co. Antrim, BT38 7DG
Tel: 028 93358000
Email: info@carrickfergus.org
Web: www.carrickfergus.org

Opening Hours

Monday to Friday, 9.00 to 5.00
Saturday, 10.00 to 5.00; closed Sunday
Admission is free

Facilities

Access and facilities for disabled
Museum shop

How to Find Us

Located in the city centre of Carrickfergus.

Carrickfergus Museum and Civic Centre was officially opened on 24 March 2005. The museum's purpose is to interpret the long and distinguished history of the town and surrounding area from the earliest times to the present day. This excellent new facility was developed with assistance from the Heritage Lottery Fund, and provides access to a wide range of interesting and important Carrickfergus-related artefacts never before displayed collectively in the Carrickfegus Borough Council area. Carrickfergus Museum is a partner in the Mid-Antrim Museum Service with Larne, Newtownabbey and Ballymena Councils.

The main display gallery shows artefacts belonging to the Council's own civic collection as well as important material on loan from both private and national collections. There are several "hands on" interactive facilities giving a fun as well as an informative angle to the displays.

"The Gallery" is the temporary gallery providing a programme of temporary exhibitions. Some exhibitions will be produced by the museum, others will be brought in as touring exhibitions from other museums and institutions.

The museum's education room provides the base for curriculum-linked education programmes, which includes workshops for schools and associated resource materials. It also provides an operational base for outreach work with the local community.

The Community Archive gives the public the opportunity to display their own information, stories, photographs, documents and newspapers as well as adding to the collection.

Carrickfergus Museum

Cavan County Museum

Contact Information

Virginia Road
Ballyjamesduff, Co. Cavan
Tel: 049 8544070
Email: ccmuseum@eircom.net
Web: www.cavanmuseum.ie

Opening Hours

Tuesday to Saturday, 10.00 to 5.00
June to September, Sunday, 2.00 to
6.00; closed Monday
Admission fees: **Adult,** €3.00;
Senior/Student, €1.50;
Family, €8.00

Facilities

Coffee shop
Gift shop
Wheelchair access

How to Find Us

Located just outside Ballyjamesduff,
Co. Cavan.

Cavan County Museum, which opened to the public in 1996, is situated in Ballyjamesduff, in the restored nineteenth-century Poor Clare Convent with spacious grounds and gardens. The museum traces the history of County Cavan from earliest times to the present day. The collection comprises archaeological finds from the Stone Age to the Middle ages, includes the three-faced pre-Christian Corleck Head and a 1,000-year-old dugout boat. There is also a fine display of eighteenth-, nineteenth- and twentieth-century costume, galleries on folk life, the Gaelic Athletic Association and Camogie Association.

The museum is fully committed to creating an awareness of the immense value of heritage in terms of identity, culture, tourism, children's education and a sense of community and national pride.

With an active Education Programme, the museum caters not only for children and young adults, but also for groups such as senior citizens, young mothers and people with special needs or disabilities.

This award-winning museum is a creative resource centre for schools and special interest groups. Guided tours are available on request.

Temporary Exhibition Space

The Temporary Exhibition space is located on the top floor of the museum.

Over a twelve-month period this space accommodates up to ten varying exhibitions which show the multiplicity of interests in County Cavan. This gallery responds to public demand for historical arts and cultural events and the staff are constantly updating their knowledge in order to best respond to the various interest of our clients.

This gallery also reflects the degree to which the Recreation and Amenities Service of Cavan County

Bronze Age casting

council work closely together with museum staff to bring a varied and interesting programme to attract new people to the museum on an ongoing basis.

Coleraine Museum

Contact Information

Coleraine Burough Council
66 Portstewart Rd.
Coleraine, Co. Derry
Tel: 028 70347234
E-mail: helen.perry@colerainebc.gov.uk
Web: www.colerainebc.gov.uk

Opening Hours

Telephone or see website for details.
Admission is free

Facilities

Access and facilities for disabled

How to Find Us

Located in the Coleraine Town Hall
in the city centre.

Watercolour by Hugh Thomson (1860–1920) (study for Shakespeare's As You Like It*)*

Situated on the River Bann, eight km from the sea and with an impressive history dating back to Ireland's earliest known settlers, Coleraine today is a major gateway to the popular Causeway Coast area.

Over 9,000 years old, Mountsandel (now a suburb of Coleraine) is the site of the earliest known settlement in Ireland. The area was a rich source of salmon with easy access to the sea and the fertile valley of the Bann river. Mountsandel occupies a strategic position above a ford in the river. Since that time there has been continuous activity in the area — notably the Vikings used the Bann as a "highway" and the Normans built the first bridge across the Bann at Coleraine.

The Coleraine Museum collection is made accessible through temporary exhibitions and an events programme in Coleraine Town Hall. The collection includes Neolithic archaeology, domestic textiles, clothing, artworks, illuminated addresses, rare books, maps and more.

Highlights from the Collection

Highlights include a 1702 Coleraine Mace, 1720 Knox Goblet, Ferrara Sword, Gribbon Family Linen Seals and Archives, Hugh Thomson collection of nearly 800 watercolours, drawings and books from his personal library, and photographic collections of Walker, Diamond & Glassey of local communities and their place.

Coleraine Mace, 1702

Donegal County Museum

Contact Information

High Road
Letterkenny, Co. Donegal
Tel: 074 9124613
Email: museum@donegalcoco.ie
Web: www.donegal.ie

Opening Hours

Monday to Friday, 10.00 to 4.30,
Closed for lunch 12.30 to 1.00
Saturday, 1.00 to 4.30
Admission is free.

Facilities

Wheelchair access

How to Find Us

Located on the High Road, opposite
the Revenue and the Orchard Inn.

Donegal County Museum first opened to the public in 1987. In the first phase of development the museum was housed in what was once the Warden's house of the Letterkenny Workhouse, built in 1843.

The role of Donegal County Museum is to collect, record, preserve, communicate and display, for the use and enjoyment of the widest community possible, the material evidence and associated information of the history of Donegal.

Donegal County Museum preserves and celebrates the collective memory of the county and its communities, through the preservation, display and interpretation of artefacts. It aims to make the community live through the objects. It aims to be a dynamic, social, cultural institution which serves all of its communities — adult, child, unwaged, elderly, disabled, as well as people of all creeds and opinions — and to have an overt sense of purpose which will encourage all to learn and to understand the past through museum objects.

In order to achieve these aims the museum contains two exhibition galleries, a workshop, a storage area and offices.

Display at Donegal County Museum

The museum develops and cares for a comprehensive collection of original artefacts relating to the history of County Donegal in the areas of archaeology, geology, natural history, social and political history and folklife. The museum has a workshop and storage facility where artefacts are preserved and stored under the appropriate environmental conditions.

A series of temporary exhibitions are held each year in the ground floor gallery on various topics. The exhibition in the first floor gallery covers topics in Donegal history from the Stone Age to the twentieth century.

Display at Donegal County Museum

Down County Museum

Contact Information

The Mall, Downpatrick,
Co. Down, BT30 GAH
Tel: 028 44615218
Email: museum@downdc.gov.uk
Web: www.downcountymuseum.com

Opening Hours

Monday to Saturday, 10.00 to 5.00
Saturday and Sunday, 1.00 to 5.00
Admission is free

Facilities

Restaurant
Gift shop
Wheelchair access

How to Find Us

The museum is located on the Mall,
English Street, Downpatrick and is
within easy walking distance of the
town centre.

Down County Museum collects, conserves and exhibits artefacts relating to the history of County Down from the earliest times until today. Its aim is to enhance appreciation of the history, culture and environment of the county through the organisation of exhibitions, activities and events which are informative, accessible and relevant to the local community and visitors.

The Ballybrannagh Quilt

The museum is located in the historic buildings of the eighteenth-century County Gaol of Down. The

Living History at Down County Museum

Down Gaol was opened in 1796 and until its closure in 1830 housed many thousands of prisoners. The museum's new online prisoners database allows visitors to search for details of prisoners.

In addition to incarcerating many people for very minor offences, the gaol held 1798 rebels captured after the battles of Saintfield and Ballynahinch, and the United Irishman, Thomas Russell, executed for his role in the abortive rebellion of 1803.

The gaol was also a convict gaol and many hundreds of transportees were imprisoned there prior to their journey to the convict colonies of New South Wales. The museum began a programme of restoring the gaol buildings in 1981, and now visitors to the site can see the conditions in which the prisoners were kept, visit restored cells complete with displays on individual prisoners, and stroll through the gaol courtyards which today are the scene of lively events and re-enactments. The museum's permanent exhibitions include galleries dedicated to the history of the county, the story of the Norman conquest of Down and the history of the gaol.

A programme of temporary exhibitions deals with everything from the Victorians to local artists.

Saint Patrick

In 1984, the museum opened its first public gallery with an exhibition about St Patrick. This explained, in a very simple way, the story of the real St Patrick. The exhibitions may have changed since then but the museum now holds an important collection of Early Christian objects, including carved stone cross slabs on loan from the Select Vestry of Saul Church.

In addition to the artefacts of that period, the museum is interested in other material relating to St Patrick, such as works of art, commemorative material and publications.

Downpatrick now hosts major celebrations on St Patrick's Day each year, with one of the largest parades in Ireland. It is one of the busiest dates in our events calendar, when we generally welcome between 2,000-3,500 visitors.

Education

Down County Museum runs an award winning education service which complements National Curriculum work in the areas of history, cultural heritage, environmental

geography, English, art, design and technology.

The Community Education Officer and Education Assistant are happy to answer any queries visitors have and are available to assist with booking.

This bronze sculpture by Oisin Kelly incorporates the words in Irish of the second verse of the hymn known as "St Patrick's Breastplate". In the centre is a "chi rho" (XP), an early Christian symbol formed of the first two letters, in Greek, of the name of Christ.

"The museum is a torpedo moving through time, its head the ever-advancing present, its tail the ever-receding past . . ."

— Alfred Barr

Downpatrick Railway Museum

Contact Information

Market Street, Downpatrick,
Co. Down, BT30 6LZ
Tel: 077 90802049 / 028 44615779
Email: downtrains@yahoo.co.uk
Web: www.downrail.co.uk

Opening Hours

St Patrick's Day, Easter, May Day,
Summer weekends, Halloween (last
October weekend) Christmas (first
three December weekends)
Admission fees: Adult, £4.50stg;
Seniors and Children, £3.50stg

Facilities

Restaurant
Gift shop
Wheelchair access

How to Find Us

Located on the Downpatrick-New-
castle Road, beside Bus Station.

This railway is Northern Ireland's only standard gauge (i.e. full size) heritage railway and is based in the county town of Down. The railway connects various sites of Down's Christian heritage, such as Inch Abbey and a grave of a Viking King, Magnus Barefoot. The Downpatrick & Co. Down Railway is a not-for-profit society as well as a registered charity and museum. There currently is a membership of just under 200 people from all over the world.

The railway has in use, and on display, a number of steam and diesel locomotives. Several of these are owned by the museum; the remainder are owned by private individuals or other organisations and are on loan to the railway. Most of these are operational, although at any given time some might be withdrawn for overhaul or repair.

Entirely staffed by volunteers, the railway has been painstakingly rebuilt by people giving up their Wednesdays, Saturdays, Sundays or even Thursday evenings! Unlike many other Northern Ireland attractions, members of the public can and are positively encouraged to shape the future direction of the railway.

Highlights from the Collection

Highlights from the collection include vintage wooden bodied carriages — the only ones that can be operated in Northern Ireland — and vintage steam engines.

The steam train passing underneath Down Cathedral.

Fermanagh County Museum

Contact Information

Enniskillen Castle & Museums,
Castle Barracks, Enniskillen,
Co. Fermanagh, N. Ireland, BT74 7HL
Tel: 028 66325000
Email: castle@fermanagh.gov.uk
Web: www.enniskillencastle.co.uk

Opening Hours

Monday, 2.00 to 5.00; Tuesday to
Friday, 10.00 to 5.00; Saturday, 2.00
to 5.00 (May to September only);
Sunday, 2.00 to 5.00 (July and
August only)
Sunday and Holidays, 11.00 to 5.00
Admission fees: **Adult**, £2.75stg;
Children, £1.65stg; Family, £7.15stg

Facilities

Gift shop
Wheelchair access

How to Find Us

Enniskillen Castle and Museums
are located on the Wellington Road,
Enniskillen within easy walking
distance of the town centre.

The museum is located within and around the historic Enniskillen Castle and was established in 1976 by Fermanagh District Council. The museum collections reflect Fermanagh's history, culture and environment. One of the aims of the museum is to enlarge these collections to cover as many aspects of Fermanagh's culture as possible and a primary concern is the long-term preservation of these collections for future generations.

Throughout the year, the museum provides a changing exhibition programme, covering a wide diversity of subjects, of local as well as general interest. It organises many different kinds of events, including lectures, living history events, craft demonstrations, storytelling, poetry and prose readings, various commemorative events and many types of family entertainment programmes during the summer, at Christmas and at Hallowe'en. Its education programmes meet the needs of those in formal education as well as providing resources for lifelong learning.

Tinplate Mechanical Tractor

Fermanagh County Museum's award-winning exhibitions cover the prehistory and natural history of

The Watergate, Enniskillen Castle

Fermanagh, the county's traditional rural life, local crafts and the celebrated pottery at Belleek. Additional displays within Enniskillen Castle trace the long and complex history of this building from its original use as a stronghold of the local Gaelic Maguire chieftains to its later use as a Plantation castle and military barracks.

Highlights from the Collection

The museum's mission is to collect and preserve significant material and information about Fermanagh's history, culture and environment and, through its exhibitions, educational activities and events, to promote an appreciation of Fermanagh's cultural richness among local people and visitors to the county.

At present the collections consist of around 8,000 artefacts as well as a large amount of photographic material and oral history recordings and transcripts. Fermanagh County Museum has recently purchased some fine examples of nineteenth and twentieth century art and craftsmanship for the enjoyment of present and future generations. These include four important examples of Belleek Pottery, a rare First Period Scotch Whisky barrel used originally in a public house, a coffee set decorated with Celtic animal interlace and designed in the 1920s, a First Period three-stranded basket and a very delicate Second Period covered basket. The Museum has an extensive collection of archaeological, historical, fine art, decorative/applied art and folklife artefacts as well as a substantial photographic and oral history collection.

New Developments/Future Plans

"Connecting Peoples, Places & Heritage" is a cross-border collaboration between Cavan and Fermanagh County Museums. The project aims to foster cross-border links between schools and youth groups. The project runs six heritage trails. The Prehistory Trail allows children to visit tombs built by Neolithic people. The Early Christianity Trail visits

Devenish Island and Drumlane Abbey. The Famine Trail brings children back to the nineteenth century and traces the plight of people in pre-famine times and the cataclysmic impact of the famine in 1845. The Industrial Revolution trail looks at a nationwide phenomenon in the context of

"Women of the World" at Enniskillen Castle Fun Day

County Fermanagh and Cavan. The Creation of the Border Trail directly confronts the issues surrounding the modern partition of Ireland. The trails are available to all schools and youth groups and are free of charge.

Educational Programmes

The Museum prides itself on the high quality of its education service. It provides worksheets, clipboards and all materials required for your visit. The service has a "direct teaching" approach so teachers and group leaders can relax while museum staff present the programmes, or they can provide guidance materials to help teachers and leaders conduct their own classes.

"A painter told me that nobody could draw a tree without in some sort becoming a tree; or draw a child by studying the outlines of its form merely . . . but by watching for a time his motions and plays, the painter enters into his nature and can then draw him at every attitude . . ."

— Ralph Waldo Emerson

The Glebe House and Gallery

Contact Information

Church Hill
Letterkenny, Co. Donegal
Tel: 074 9137071

Opening Hours

Open daily from start of June to end of September; closed Fridays in June and September
Admission is free to gallery. House by guided tour only: Adults, €2.75; Seniors, €2.00; Children, €1.25; Family, €7.00

Facilities

Coffee shop
Gift shop
Wheelchair acceess (ground floor only)

How to find us

Located beside Lough Gartan, east of Glenveagh National Park.

Glebe House, originally known as St Columb's, was bulit in the Regency style in 1828 as the rectory to St Columba's (Church of Ireland). The house was eventually sold and, after renovations, opened in 1898 as St Columb's Hotel, taking guests for the salmon and trout fishing in spring and summer and for the shooting in the autumn. Apart from the years 1916–1922, when the hotel was taken over for a short while by the IRA and later by the Royal Irish Constabulary, the hotel was open every day until the death of its owner, Mrs Kitty Johnstone, in 1950. It was then run by her daughter until it was acquired by the painter Derek Hill.

Interior of the Gallery

Derek Hill's love of landscape painting was matched by his interest in portraiture and over the years he painted a wide range of subjects. His paintings of Tory Island inspired a number of islanders to paint and the "Tory Island School" has now achieved international acclaim in its own right. In 1981 Derek Hill donated St Columb's, its contents and gardens to the nation. Hill's studio and guesthouse were transformed into the Glebe Gallery, displaying items from the Derek Hill collection, as well as providing a location for travelling exhibitions. The house and gardens are displayed in an informal manner, as though Derek Hill was still in residence. In recognition of his unfailing support of the arts in Ireland, Hill was awarded an honorary doctorate by Trinity College Dublin, and made an honorary citizen of Ireland in 1998. He died in London in 2000.

The Kitchen at Glebe House

Highlights of the Collection

Works in the Hall and Morning Room include *Study of Fruit* by Louis le Brocquy; a framed square of Willow Boughs wallpaper, designed by William Morris in 1897; a display of Victorian and Edwardian postcards; and a loving-cup, which is a fine example of Wemyss Ware.

In the Dining Room are four paintings by Sir Edwin Landseer; a mid-nineteenth-century inlaid dining table, which depicts the various arts; tiles in the mantelpiece by William de Morgan, and a painting of the Dromara Hills in Co. Down by the Antrim artist Basil Blackshaw.

In the Drawing Room and Japanese Room are a display cabinet with decorative pieces from the nineteenth and early twentieth centuries;

the painting *Evening Thames at Chiswick* by Victor Pasmore; a Chinese cabinet with ceramic insets; a large painting by Derek Hill, *Donegal, Late Harvest*; and nineteenth-century Japanese woodblock prints hanging on bamboo-printed paper.

In the Morris Bedroom, there is wallpaper by William Morris called Golden Lily; a mahogany half-tester bed; and a painting by John Bratby called *Jean in Bed with Jaundice*.

Elsewhere in the house are paintings by Picasso, Kokoshka, James Dixon and others.

New Developments

There will be three temporary exhibitions during the summer of 2006. Recent exhibitions include pre-Colombian art, Henry Moore and "Making Time".

Glebe House Gallery

Gray Printers' Museum

Contact Information

49 Main Street
Strabane, Co. Tyrone BT82 8AU
Tel: 028 71884094
Web: www.strabanedc.com

Opening Hours

Open year round, Tuesday to
Saturday 11.00 to 5.00;
Admission is free

Facilities

Disabled access

How to Find Us

Located on Strabane's Main Street
with nearby Pay and Display park-
ing.

Gray Printers' Museum is located in Strabane, Co. Tyrone and is under the management of Strabane District Council. The museum building was formerly a print and stationery shop and it had a long association with printing, something that appeared to have been particularly strong in Strabane since the eighteenth century. An early newspaper, *The Strabane Morning Post*, was printed in what is now the museum from 1812 to 1837.

The museum was established in the mid-1990s when the stationery business closed down. Many of the museum's holdings were acquired from a private collector, Mr Dunbar of Newtownstewart, and the artefacts in the collection reflect the everyday life of the people of west Ulster in the nineteenth and early twentieth centuries. House-hold items, agricultural tools, shopping articles and war memorabilia help to make up a sizable portion of the 2,000-plus artefacts in the museum's collection.

Viewing Gallery in Museum

In recent years much emphasis has been placed on collecting other aspects of local heritage and the museum is currently hosting a photographic exhibition on images of the district from the early decades of the twentieth century. This Cooper Collection was originally amassed in Strabane and is now in the keeping of the Public Record Offices of Northern Ireland. Railway memorabilia and images have added substantially to the collection recently while much was collected in the recent past on entertainment and music, with the Clipper Charlton showband exhibition proving inspirational in collecting locally. Work is currently underway in cataloguing local government and genealogical information and this will add substantially to the museum's holdings.

Early Church Bell on display

Green Lane Museum

Contact Information

Weaving Shed
Roe Valley Country Park
Limavady, Co. Derry
Tel: 028 77760304
Email: eileen.magee@limavady.gov.uk
Web: www.limavady.gov.uk

Opening Hours

Daily May to September, 1.00 to 5.00
Admission is free

Facilities

Wheelchair access

How to Find Us

Located in the Roe Valley Country
Park, one mile outside Limavady.

The Green Lane Museum explores the nineteenth and twentieth century rural heritages of the Roe Valley. It has been built up by a steady flow of donations from local people. On display are examples of local trades, life on the farm, and working in the kitchen. Also included is a feature on linen, one of the key stories along with hydroelectricity. The musuem is an old weaving shed, one of the many listed remains of industrial heritage throughout the park. Local stories are enhanced through temporary exhibitions.

Highlights from the Collection

Highlights include an 1813 map of County Londonderry by G. Sampson; 1698 estate maps of Newtown Limavady; Hunters Bakers cart; Ballykelly airbase items including wreckage; the Buchanan photo collection; a postcard collection; a tumbling body plough; a mobilette milking machine; and a W. Wallace delivery bicycle.

Hands-on activity at the Green Lane Museum

"To be ignorant of what happened before you were born . . . is to live the life of a child for ever."

— *Cicero*

Larne Museum, Carnegie Centre and Arts

Contact Information

2 Victoria Road
Larne, Co. Antrim, BT40 1RN
Tel: 028 28729482
Web: www.larne.gov.uk

Opening Hours

Open September to Easter, Monday to Friday, 12.30 to 5.00; Easter to August, Monday to Saturday, 12.30 to 5.00
Admission is free

Facilities

Wheelchair access

How to Find Us

Located in the town centre of Larne, Co. Antrim.

The newly opened Carnegie Centre houses Larne Museum, a termporary exhibition gallery, auditorium and education centre. The Carnegie Centre gives a new lease of life to the Carnegie Library, originally opened to the public in 1906, which has been beautifully restored and renovated with many of its original features remaining intact. The museum charts Larne Borough's maritime, agricultural, industrial and social history through a range of exhibits and interactive features. The temporary gallery has a wide variety of exhibitions throughout the year, including historic costume and art exhibitions.

equipment on display which reveal the history of farming in the area. Larne's strong maritime connection

Entrance to the Larne Museum

is displayed through a variety of objects relating to the first roll-on roll-off ferries, the Royal Navy and the *Princeses Victoria* disaster. The history of the Home Rule crisis, gun running and the First and Second World Wars are revealed by a wealth of objects in the "War and Conflict" section of the museum. Visitors can access personal accounts and memories through oral history listening posts and browse through photographs in the community archive.

Education Programmes

The museum's education programme started in February 2006 with "Home Life in Larne during the Last Hundred Years" for Key Stage 1 pupils. "Children at Play in Victorian Times" will be available for Key Stage 2 pupils in May 2006.

Larne Pottery Jug

Highlights from the Collection

Larne Museum has an excellent collection of agricultural tools and

Millennium Court
Arts Centre

Contact Information

William Street, Portadown,
Northern Ireland BT62 3NX
Tel: 00 44 28 3839 4415
E-mail: info@millenniumcourt.org
Web: www.millenniumcourt.org

Opening Hours

Tuesday to Thursday, 10.00 to 9.00
Monday, Friday and Saturday,
10.00 to 5.00
Admission is free

Facilities

Café
Gift shop
Wheelchair access

How to Find Us

Located in the town centre of
Portadown on William Street, just
off Market Street.

Millennium Court Arts Centre houses two purpose-built gallery spaces and has been described as one of Ireland's premier art spaces. In addition, the centre includes a verbal arts room with a visual and verbal archive library, and a multimedia suite equipped fully with video editing and sound recording. Within the complex there is also a darkroom, visual arts workshop and artist-in-residence suite, all of which combine to create a vibrant and unique environment in which to cultivate and enhance the cultural environment of the community.

Since opening MCAC has facilitated the commissioning of new work with more than a dozen projects completed to date. This year the centre will continue that interest by encouraging local, national and international artists to respond to notions of place and space. "Interrogating Contested Spaces in Post-Conflict Society: Collaboration in Verbal and Visual Art" is just one example where noted writers, poets and visual artists collaborate to produce a body of new work reflecting on and re-examining current complex issues surrounding urbanisation, gentrification, loss, trauma, memory and dislocation.

While keen to engage with national and international artists, MCAC recognises the importance of developing a local creative visual

Gallery 1

milieu. The Portadown Visual Artists Society will once again hold their annual showcase this year. Young emerging artists from the area are also represented. Overall, MCAC's programme is dynamic, multifaceted, and wide ranging. It aspires to open up the public's imagination to as many creative art forms as possible while simultaneously offering discussion and exploration through its innovative Education and Outreach programmes.

Highlights from the Collection

MCAC does not have a permanent collection. Instead the focus is on the commissioning of new, innovative challenging work by local, national and international artists, with more than a dozen projects completed to date. This policy lends itself to the continuing engagement with contemporary art from diverse media such as painting, sculpture, print-making, textiles, multimedia, design and installation art. MCAC encourages artists to respond to notions of place and space where each artist produces a new body of new work reflecting on and re-examining these complex issues. It is a policy to give each artist the opportunity of showcasing their work in a white cube where every assistance is give in developing their artistic and professional practice. The Arts Centre also houses selected works donated by previously exhibited artists.

New Developments

In 2004, MCAC decided to position itself firmly in contemporary design by focusing on the promotion of design in all its forms, including architecture, furniture, photography, contemporary textiles and innovative craft. This new curatorial focus has begun to take shape in the form of the shows chosen for the forthcoming year, thereby providing a showcase for craft and design practices. This direction is due in no small part

to the strength of shows like "From the Edge — Contemporary textiles" and the upcoming "Frank Gehry, Architect: Designs for Museums". This practice firmly places the broad concept of contemporary design within the curatorial programme with four shows showcasing design this year; Frank Gehry (architecture), UBIFHIE (furniture and photography), and "40 Shades of Green" (contemporary craft). Each show will highlight this important and innovative field.

Educational Programmes

The Millennium Court Arts Centre is committed to developing innovative education activities and projects for diverse audiences. During each exhibition the centre delivers a regular series of talks and events and specific outreach activities for schools

Participant in Open Art Days

and community groups. The Education Department invites people of all backgrounds to explore, participate, experience and enjoy contemporary art practices through exhibition talks, guided tours, lectures and seminars, artist-led sessions and hands-on workshops. MCAC believes the most significant objective for all participants is their creative experience. As one of the foremost pioneers of creative thinking in Northern Ireland in both rural and urban areas, MCAC aims to have a varied and wide selection of accessible workshops that are both traditional and experimental. MCAC recognises the potential for creative achievement and continues to strive to offer a high-level education programme in an environment in which everyone is encouraged to express and develop their creativity.

for 2006 include readings from esteemed poet Cathal Ó Searchaigh, singer/songwriter Brian Kennedy and a presentation from Bluechrome Publishing. The centre's Multimedia Department delivers a programme that promotes multimedia and new technology, advancing excellence in artistic creation in new and emerging art forms. MCAC recognises the need to take a distinctive and challenging position regarding the

Novelist Glenn Patterson reading from his latest work

Additional Comments

MCAC has a very strong Verbal Arts Programme which includes all aspects of the spoken word. Events highlight verbal arts locally, regionally, nationally and internationally. The programme delivers a broad spectrum of verbal arts that will "alter perceptions" and encourage debate that will spark and inspire creativity. Upcoming events

events, concerts and exhibitions, working with artists and musicians whose practice clearly shows a forward and contemporary take on new media art forms and presentation. It wants to foster a change in attitudes and beliefs on what is art while engaging the viewers' curiosity. The aim is to develop the creative potential of individuals and communities using MCAC's resources.

Museum of the Master Saddler

Contact Information

Corlough
Co. Cavan
Tel: 049 9523956
Email: info@robsteinke.com
Web: www.robsteinke.com

Opening Hours

By appointment.
Admission fees: **Adult**, €4.00;
Children, €2.00; Concessions, €3.00

Facilities

Coffee facilities
Gift shop
Wheelchair access

How to Find Us

Take the Enniskillen Road out of Ballinamore to Corlough cross road. Turn left and follow the signs.

The Museum of the Master Saddler is the world's only museum devoted exclusively to the craft of the saddler and harness maker. Its curator, Rob Steinke, served his apprenticeship with the Royal Saddler, Keith Luxford, and at the world famous Cordwainers Leather College in London. He later set up his own business specialising in custom made-to-measure saddlery and driving harnesses, which he exported throughout the world. During this time he also exhibited and demonstrated his craft at some of the most prestigious shows in Europe, including the Royal Welsh, Smith's Lawn in Windsor, and the Irish National Driving Championships in the grounds of Birr Castle.

The museum traces the craft of the saddler from the earliest times through to use in farming, transport, the military and on to modern day activities such as racing, hunting, showing and carriage driving for

Hand-stitched brown harness

Highlights from the Collection

Highlights include an 1880 Victorian Garden Chaise, a 1910 cart with a basketwork body, a 1920s ladies' side saddle, a display of saddle trees and step-by-step saddle making, a collection of miniature pony driving harnesses, examples of over 70 different types of leather and horse collars, both traditional straw and modern day rubber.

Hand-made harness for miniature pony

New Developments/Future Plans

The museum is planning to create a series of historical saddles, including Roman, Norman and Medieval. It is also planning to make a DVD on the craft of the master saddler.

pleasure. The museum is open by appointment so that visitors can be given a guided tour.

Naughton Gallery at Queen's

Contact Information

Lanyan Building
Queen's University
University Road
Belfast BT7 1NN
Tel: 028 90973580
Email: art@qub.ac.uk
Web: www.naughtongallery.org

Opening Hours

Monday to Saturday, 11.00 to 4.00
Admission is free

Facilities

Gift shop
Wheelchair access

How to Find Us

Located on the campus of Queen's
University in Belfast.

John Luke, Connswater Bridge, *1934*

Since 2001, The Naughton Gallery has become one of Belfast's most sought-after and exciting visual arts platforms, featuring a rolling programme of works from the University's own collection, touring exhibitions and shows by local and international artists. The Naughton Gallery is a registered museum.

The Naughton Gallery presents up to six exhibitions per year and also co-ordinates commissions of new art works for Queen's University. The University's extensive art collection comprises gifts, bequests and purchases since the foundation of Queen's College in 1845. The wide range of works include paintings, prints, works on paper, sculpture, furniture, metalwork and silver. The collection is on display throughout the University with an impressive hang of over sixty portraits in the Great Hall.

The Naughton Gallery

Past exhibitions have included solo shows by John Keane, T.P. Flanagan and Tai-Shan Schierenberg and an installation by sound artist Scanner as well as historical explorations such as "The Classical Feminine" and a retrospective of Georgina Moutray Kyle. The gallery has also been transformed by "street illuminations" from Calcutta and Day of the Dead crafts from Mexico.

The gallery welcomes 13,000 annual visitors including a significant number of international tourists. For further information, please visit the gallery's new website at www.naughtongallery.org.

Highlights from the Collection

The University's extensive art collection comprises gifts, bequests and purchases since the foundation of Queen's College in 1845. The impressive range of works includes

The Naughton Gallery

paintings, prints, works on paper, sculpture, furniture, metalwork and silver. The collection includes paintings by Irish artists including Luke, Lavery, and le Brocquy as well as contemporary works.

New Developments

Coming soon is a pioneering interactive display of the University's silver collection.

Educational Programmes

The gallery has a dedicated Education and Outreach Officer who creates greater access to the visual arts for schools and community groups and, in particular, young people. Activities include visual and multi-media artists working with schools, co-ordinated visits to the gallery and the creation of exhibitions by young people themselves.

Some of the projects have included making prints, writing haiku and composing music, recording sound-scapes, modelling skeletons and em-broidering flags with help from in-ternational artists from all over the world.

Every year, thousands of people gain access to the visual arts through the Naughton Gallery Outreach Pro-gramme.

William Conor, Ready for Action

"There are few delights in any life so high and rare as the subtle and strong delight of sovereign art and poetry . . . to have beheld or heard the greatest works of any great painter or musician is a possession added to the best things of life."

— Algernon Charles Swinburne

Sheelin Irish Lace Museum

Contact Information

Bellanaleck
Enniskillen, Co. Fermanagh
Tel: 028 66348052
Email: info@irishlacemuseum.com
Web: www.irishlacemuseum.com

Opening Hours

By appointment.
Admission fees: Adults, £2.50stg;
Children, £1.50stg; Groups of 15
or more, £1.50stg

Facilities

Gift shop
Wheelchair access

How to Find Us

Located in Bellanaleck, four miles
from Enniskillen.

The Lace Museum has approximately 700 exhibits. All the five main types of lace made in Ireland are represented in the collection – Youghal, Inishmacsaint, Crochet, Limerick and Carrickmacross. All the laces date from between 1850 and 1900. On display we have several wedding gowns, veils, shawls, parasols, collars, baby bonnets, christening gowns, flounces, jackets and many more items. The museum traces the history of lace-making in Ireland and conveys to the visitor the importance of the industry to Ireland as a whole and to Irish women in particular. The entrance to the museum houses the lace shop where we have hundreds of antique laces for sale. This is one of the very few places in Ireland to see and buy antique lace.

Irish crochet wedding dress c.1890–1900

Highlights from the Collection

The highlight of the collection are the wedding gowns, but there is also the largest collection of Inishmacsaint needlelace on show anywhere in Ireland. Inishmacsaint lace was made in Co. Fermanagh and the museum was lucky to be able to purchase it from the family whose great-grandfather started the industry in Benmore Rectory, Co. Fermanagh. On show in the museum is a spectacular Youghal flounce which was worked in 1880. Our most recent purchase was a collection of garments and laces made at the Lissadell Lace School in Sligo.

Close-up of lace high collar

Tower Museum and La Trinidad Valencera

Contact Information

Union Hall Place
Derry BT48 6LU
Tel: 028 9071372411
Email: johnny.kurray@derrycity.gov.uk
Web:www.derrycity.gov.uk/museums

Opening Hours

Open Monday to Friday,
10.00 to 4.30.
Admission: Adults, £3.00stg; Group
rates available.

Facilities

Wheelchair access

How to Find Us

Located in the city centre opposite
the Guildhall.

The Tower Museum is the venue for a fascinating exhibition of an Armada shipwreck, *La Trinidad Valencera*, which puts on display many of the artefacts recovered from the sunken ship. This vessel was one of the largest ships in the Armada fleet and foundered in Kinnagoe Bay, just along the north coast of Donegal, during a violent storm in 1588. The excavation was one of the first underwater archaeological ventures of its kind and has supplied a stunning collection of material through revolutionary techniques invented to excavate, chart and recover the material from the ship.

The top of the Tower Museum (level 5) provides the only open air viewing facility in the heart of the city centre with stunning panoramic views of the inner city and river Foyle. Moving from the outdoor brightness to a moody and theatrical level 4, the visitor continues with the period of history that tells the story of the ill-fated Armada voyage. Exit staircases with graphics

Entrance to the Tower Museum

and sound draw visitors further into the story and onto level 3 to the seabed of Kinnagoe Bay where *La Trinidad Valencera* was shipwrecked. This level has original excavation footage from 1971 and outlines the pioneering underwater archaeology that was first tested in the waters of the North West of Ireland. The City of Derry Sub-Aqua Club, who found the wreck, tell their story along with the poignant stories of the Armada survivors. The double height space and large-scale graphics bring a feeling of depth to this evocative space.

This theme is continued in level 2 where an excavation mock-up of the seabed brings

Display at the Museum

together a corresponding grid and replica objects. This floor has an open display of a cannon retrieved from the wreck, accessible in a dedicated alcove display area. The cannon is also the centrepiece of the newly constructed welcome visual for the Museum. It is situated in a showcase display area of a large window that creates an unusual and unique external welcome feature for the Museum.

Level 1 is the interactive area for families and visitors with hands-on interactive areas bringing to life the science of excavation and the knowledge of the underwater world of archaeology and the intricacies of conservation.

A new reception area will create a welcoming space for visitors and in 2006 will also direct visitors to the refurbished Story of Derry Exhibi-

tion fitted with new display cases, enhanced visitor orientation and a range of updated audiovisuals.

The Tower Museum is located within the city's historic walls and has won four major awards since its

Display showing diving and excavation

opening in October 1992. These include the Irish Museum of the Year Award 1993, The British Airways Tourism Endeavour Award 1993, the National Heritage IBM UK Museum of the Year Award 1994 and Special Commendation European Museum of the Year Award in 1994.

New Developments

The refurbished Story of Derry exhibition will re-open in June 2006.

A curator working on one of the displays

"*I have but one lamp by which my feet are guided, and that is the lamp of experience. I know no way of judging of the future but by the past.*"

— *Edward Gibbon*

Ulster American Folk Park

Contact Information

2 Mellon Road, Castletown
Omagh, Co. Tyrone, BT78 5QY
Tel: 028 82243292
Email: uafp.info@magni.org.uk
Web: www.folkpark.com

Opening Hours

October to March, Monday to Friday,
10.30 to 5.00, closed weekends and
holidays; April to September,
Monday to Friday, 10.30 to 6.30
Admission: Adults, £4.50stg;
Concession, £2.50stg; Children
under five free; Group and Family
rates available upon request

Facilities

Restaurant
Gift shop
Wheelchair access

How to Find Us

Located three miles outside Omagh
on main A5 road to Strabane/Derry.

Recently awarded Best Northern Ireland Visitor Attraction, the Ulster American Folk Park is an outdoor museum of emigration which tells the story of the vast human tide of emigration to the New World over the past three centuries.

The Old World and the New World layout of the Park illustrates the various aspects of emigrant life on both sides of the Atlantic. Traditional thatched buildings, American log houses and a full-scale replica emigrant ship and the dockside gallery help to bring a bygone era back to life. Ulster and American streets with mostly original shop fronts have also been reconstructed.

Visitors can see, taste and smell the past as costumed demonstrators go about their everyday tasks in the traditional manner in authentically

Open hearth cooking in Mellon House

Ship and dockside exhibition

furnished buildings. Visitors are able to taste traditional fare and see demonstrations on traditional Irish and American crafts and agriculture including spinning, printing, blacksmithing, corn-craft and quilting.

The museum also includes an indoor exhibition which examines life in Ulster in the eighteenth and nineteenth centuries, reveals the reasons behind the exodus and shows how the emigrants adapted to and impacted on their new homelands.

There is a Centre for Migration Studies/library on site which is accessible to all visitors if they wish to research their ancestry.

The year 2006 is the thirtieth anniversary of the Museum and a full programme of special events is organised throughout the year. Some highlights include the award-winning Annual Appalachian and Bluegrass Music Festival and established favourites like the American Independence Celebrations in July and Hallowe'en Festival.

Highlights from the Collection

The collection includes over 30 ex-hibit buildings which are authenti-cally furnished including the original Mellon homestead, the birthplace of Judge Thomas Mellon, who emi-grated to Pennsylvania in 1818. There is also a full-scale replica of an emi-grant ship and dockside gallery and reconstructed Ulster and American streets from the nineteenth century. At present the museum is displaying "Threads of Emigration". This special exhibition is a display of textile-relat-ed material connecting us to those who emigrated from this island many years ago. Other collections include buildings and military, agriculture, crafts, transport and homelife objects from both Ireland and America.

New Developments

Future plans include major develop-ments in the New World site. These include reconstructing two original American buildings in storage and the acquisition of two further Ameri-can buildings.

Development plans will more clearly explain emigration over a longer period and recreate emigrant trails and settlement "hot spots" on a journey through time and space. More emigrant stories will be told which will represent an effective bal-anced interpretation through time and place.

Educational Programmes

The museum provides a compre-hensive learning programme for all ages throughout the year. This programme includes traditional craft workshops, role-play sessions, dance and music workshops and a variety of study tours.

Ulster Street

Ulster Folk and Transport Museum

Contact Information

Cultra, Holywood BT18 0EU

Tel: 028 90428428

Email: uftminfo@magni.org.uk

Web: www.uftm.org.uk

Opening Hours

Opens at 10.00 Monday to Saturday and at 11.00 on Sunday. Closing times vary from 4.00 to 6.00 according to the season.

Admission: Adults, £7.00stg; Children, £4.00stg; Concession, £4.00stg; Children under five free. Family day tickets, group discounts and annual tickets available on request

Facilities

Restaurant

Gift shop

Wheelchair access

How to Find Us

Located on the main Belfast to Bangor Road, just ten minutes outside Belfast.

The Ulster Folk and Transport Museum, recently awarded Irish Museum of the Year, is one of Ireland's foremost visitor attractions illustrating the way of life and the traditions of the people of the north of Ireland.

The Ulster Folk Museum was established by an Act of Parliament in 1958, primarily in response to the speed at which the countryside and people's way of life were changing and the need to preserve and record a heritage in danger of disappearing altogether. The museum holds materials of national and international importance. There is an obligation to ensure that the collections are accommodated, processed and preserved for posterity. The museum recognises the interrelationship between all of its diverse collections, library and archives which comprise a wide range of artefacts, structures, tape-recordings, photographs, films, books and documents.

The museum offers opportunities for visitors to experience living histo-

Costumed visitor guides and working buildings bring the museum to life

ry and explore a way of life from 100 years ago. It also illustrates the history of transport in Ireland, from its earliest forms through to present day.

At the open air Folk Museum 60 acres are devoted to illustrating the way of life of people in the early 1900s. The Folk Museum tells the story of life in early twentieth-century Ulster. A bygone era is re-created in a rural landscape of farms, cottages, traditional crops and local breeds of livestock. A typical Ulster town of the early 1900s is brought to life with homes, shops, workplaces, churches and schools. Costumed visitor guides, working buildings and exhibits, as well as the chance to

Daily traditional activities include basket making demonstrations

touch, to hear and to do, bring history to life for visitors of all ages.

The Transport Museum creatively displays Ireland's largest and most comprehensive transport collection, from horse-drawn carts to Irish-built motor cars, and from the mighty steam locomotives that graced our railways to the history of ship and aircraft building. Permanent exhibitions of international acclaim include "Irish Railway Collection", "Titanic" and the "X2 Flight Experience".

Education Programmes

Education staff at the Ulster Folk and Transport Museum have developed a varied range of resources and activities with the needs of teachers, students, community organisations and all educational programmes of study in mind. Education staff are happy to assist in planning a visit in advance and to help with any specific requirements regarding programmes, resources and facilities. Education staff have developed a wide range of programmes and activities to complement many areas of study including: history; science; technology; creative and expressive studies. Specific programmes for primary and post-primary schools include:

- Caught in the Act — A Victorian Courtroom Drama

- Life in Victorian Times — Rural and Urban Housing

- At School 100 Years Ago

- Transport Through the Ages

- Cultural Heritage and Home Economics

- Storytelling

- X2 — The Flight Experience Workshop

- Object detectives

- Traditional Arts and Craft workshops

- Numeracy trails

- Travel/Leisure and Tourism Studies

- Icebreaker sessions, team-building exercises etc. for Community Relations groups

X2 Flight Experience is an interactive exhibition exploring the history and science of flight.

Many of these programmes can be tailored to suit particular needs.

Ulster Museum

Contact Information

Botanic Gardens
Belfast BT9 5AB
Tel: 028 90383000
Email: info@magni.org.uk
Web: www.ulstermuseum.org.uk

Opening Hours

Open Monday to Friday, 10.00 to 5.00;
Saturday, 1.00 to 5.00; Sunday,
2.00 to 5.00.
Admission is free.

Facilities

Café
Gift shop
Wheelchair access

How to Find Us

Located in the Botanic Gardens, adjacent to Queen's University.

The Ulster Museum is an ideal place to explore the arts, ancient and modern history and the natural world.

Displays of art change regularly, showing the rich variety of Irish and international paintings, drawings and sculpture, and stunning displays of ceramics, glass, silver and costume from a collection of thousands of works, covering centuries of fine and decorative arts.

The history galleries tell the story of the north of Ireland, its people and their achievements from the end of the Ice Age 8,000 years ago to the present day.

The amazing diversity of the natural environment is explored in the Habitas galleries, revealed through the wonderful variety of animals and plants, minerals and fossils on show.

Gold lunula

The museum also holds around 20 temporary exhibitions each year, along with an extensive programme of lectures, workshops and events for all ages.

Highlights of the Collection

Highlights include special collections on archaeology and world cultures; the Treasures of the Armada; Irish painting, sculpture and works on paper; contemporary ceramics; Belleek collection; costume collection; and historic Irish glass.

In addition, the museum's website allows the visitor to take online tours of collections under specific themes, such as "Conflict: The Irish at War"; "Objects of Desire"; "Belleek"; "The Art of Giving"; "Images of the Ice Age"; and "Masks". See www.ulstermuseum.org.uk for more information.

Gold and ruby salamander from the Galleass Girona

New Developments

Planning work is underway for a major redevelopment of the Ulster Museum to breathe new life into a familiar and much-loved landmark, transforming the interior of the building and creating an exciting new experience for visitors.

The design concept includes a new visitor orientation facility, featuring a dramatically redesigned central courtyard and an extensive refurbishment of the museum's ground floor to enhance the spaces for temporary exhibitions, visitor access and amenities.

Central to the development is a series of new history and sciences galleries presenting the natural heritage, human history, culture and way of life from the earliest times, using the latest techniques of interpretation and discovery to engage with, and challenge, visitors.

A new Learning Zone on the ground floor, along with gallery-based learning and discovery zones, will provide unprecedented access to the themes and treasures of the museum.

Refurbishment will commence in autumn 2006 and construction work will take approximately two years, during which time the building will be closed and the collections secured offsite.

During that time the museum will be putting more of its collections on its website, and adding more online tours and e-learning activities.

The museum is also putting together a programme of outreach activities – small touring exhibitions and a series of lectures — which will be available around Northern Ireland. Staff of the Education Department will continue to offer a service to schools and community groups.

Belleek Urn, Third Period

"The moment one gives close attention to anything, even a blade of grass, it becomes a mysterious, awesome, indescribably magnificent world in itself."

— Henry Miller

W5

Contact Information

Odyssey
2 Queen's Quay
Belfast BT3 9QQ
Tel 028 9046 7700
Email: info@w5online.co.uk
Website: www.w5online.co.uk

Opening Hours

W5 is open Monday to Saturday,
10.00 to 6.00, and Sunday 12.00 to
6.00 with last admissions at 5.00.
During school term times W5
closes one hour earlier on Monday to
Thursday at 5.00 with last
admissions at 4.00.
Admission fee: Adults, £6.00stg;
Children, £4.00stg; Family, £17.00stg.

Facilities

Café
Gift shop
Wheelchair access

How to Find Us

From Belfast city centre follow signs
for the A2 Bangor onto Queen Eliza-
beth Bridge. Keep in the left lane and
immediately after crossing the River
Lagan turn left onto Queen's Island.
Follow the road for ¼ mile, the car
park is on your right.

With 160 interactive exhibits in five exhibition areas, W5 provides a unique experience as well as fun for visitors of all ages. In addition to permanent exhibits, W5 also presents a changing programme of large- and small-scale temporary exhibitions and events. W5 also has a daily programme of live science demonstrations and shows throughout the day.

W5's location at Odyssey, the Northern Ireland Millennium Landmark Project, provides spectacular views of Belfast and the River Lagan and is only a short walk from Belfast City Centre.

Exhibition Areas

WOW

Visitors can create cloud rings and watch the fire tornado rise to the ceiling.

Fit to Go

START and GET READY

This exhibit is a world of wonder for eights and under. Children can build a house, make a splash, dance to music, explore the castle and enjoy

Animated Globe in Weather Watch

make believe shopping as well as a new role-play café, real BMW Mini and new Get Ready area specially for the under-fives.

GO

Here visitors can take the tug of war challenge, get elevated on the pulley chairs, explore space, make magnets move or build and race their own K'nex car.

SEE

Here visitors can try to beat the lie detector, touch the sound wall, peer into professional microscopes, play invisible instruments, light up lasers and enjoy optical illusions.

DO

In this section visitors can design and build structures, bring robots to life, study nature's shapes and produce their own animated film.

New Developments

Fit to Go is a new multimedia space which explores the human body, genetics, diet and fitness and sustaining life in space. W5's new opinion monitor looks for opinions on a range of topical science issues such as climate change, recycling, vaccination and smoking.

Think Creative is an extension of the design and animation area. The new exhibits include further ways of exploring animation, how to use light in a dramatic and theatrical way, looking at photography and its uses in newspapers.

Weather Watch has exhibits which show the weather patterns circulating the Earth, explains highs and lows, weather around the world, how weather influences what people buy, renewable energy and opportunities to be a weather presenter.

Educational/Special Programmes

W5's interactive exhibits and education programmes have been developed specifically to support the educational curricula for both Northern Ireland and the Republic of Ireland. W5 provides a unique experience which will develop thinking skills, stimulate curiosity, increase pupils' understanding and make connections to everyday life. W5's exhibition spaces and workshops help teach the curriculum in an integrated way through maths, English, art and design, geography, science, technology and ICT, catering for all age groups from 4–18.

The Giant Lever

Heritage Outlook is a magazine that celebrates Ireland's natural and built heritage.

Produced biannually by the Heritage Council, Heritage Outlook is the only national magazine that focuses on all aspects of Irish heritage.

Heritage Outlook is a full-colour 32-page modern magazine with vibrant and varied content. Its extensive readership is diverse and influential, and includes professionals working in the heritage field, state departments, local authorities, non-governmental organisations, community groups, journalists, teachers and academics. Heritage Outlook is for anyone who has an interest in preserving Ireland's heritage. It carries news, provides analysis and offers thought-provoking articles on all aspects of heritage.

Heritage is defined as including the following areas:

- *Archaeological objects;*
- *Heritage Gardens & Parks;*
- *Architectural Heritage;*
- *Flora & Fauna;*
- *Wildlife Habitats;*
- *Landscapes;*
- *Monuments;*
- *Geology;*
- *Seascapes & wrecks;*
- *InlandWaterways*

If you would like to receive a copy of Heritage Outlook please email: mail@heritagecouncil.com

AN CHOMHAIRLE)IDHREACHTA

THE HERITAGE COUNCIL

Kilkenny, Ireland. Telephone: +353 56 7770777. Fax: +353 56 7770788.

www.heritagecouncil.ie